30

Verses

to Heal a

Mama's

Heart

30

Verses

to Heal a

Mama's

Heart

Wendy M. Hamilton

WindSpirit
PRESS

Published by WindSpirit Press
P.O. Box 270878, Flower Mound, TX 75028
www.windspiritpress.com

Trade Paperback ISBN 978-0-9797401-0-7

Cover Design by Wendy Hamilton
Original tree art by Bea Kraus

Library of Congress Cataloging-in-Publication Data
Names: Hamilton, Wendy M., author.
Title: 30 Verses to Heal a Mama's Heart/Wendy M. Hamilton.
Description: First Edition | Flower Mound, Texas: WindSpirit Press, 2017.
Identifiers: LCCN 2017917003 |ISBN 978-0-9797401-0-7 (pbk.)
LC record available at https://lccn.loc.gov/2017917003

Printed in the United States
2017–First Edition

To Kayleigh, Andrew, and Alexa,

Grateful doesn't begin to convey what I am to be your mama.
Thank you for the many ways you inspire my mama's heart.
God is good.

Contents

Section 3 – Purpose

Acknowledgments |212

Introduction and How-To Use This Devotional

When the nurse put my oldest daughter, Kayleigh, into my arms, I felt overwhelmed and insecure. I had no clue what I was doing. "Are you going to let me take her home?" I asked. The nurse mistook my question for the *When am I getting out of here?* variety and responded with, "Of course, Sweetheart, in a few days." What she didn't realize was that I was questioning her wisdom in letting me take this amazing tiny person that I loved so much out of the hospital when I had, a few minutes earlier, put my daughter's diaper on backwards. I was struggling as a first-time mom to figure out what being Kayleigh's mama meant. I wasn't sure I was able to do all that needed to be done to keep this kid alive, much less thrive in the existence God designed for her.

As I fast-forward through every age and stage of my being a mom to my kids, I find I approached God almost daily with the same questions of readiness and equipping. I wondered if I could do all that God called me to do as a mom. Too often I felt I could not do enough. However, from those sleep-deprived early years through the years where my kids began venturing out on their own, God stood by me and He strengthened me. He heard my cries. He felt the breaking of my mama's heart. He calmed my anxiety and removed my fears. He was and is my Source.

This devotional is a collection of 30 verses for the mama's heart. A mama is *any* woman who finds herself with an incredible love and instructive and caregiver purpose for another person given to her by God. That person does not necessarily have to be her biological child. A mama could be a biological or adopted mom, or a spiritual mom which includes stepmoms, aunts, and other women God gives to a person to help them as they take next steps with Him.

If you were drawn to this book then likely you are a mama, want to be a mama, or you have a mama's heart and God has equipped you with the desire to help others see Him. Or perhaps you thought of your own mama—biological, adopted, or spiritual. Either way, you have a connection to the mama's heart.

These select verses of Scripture help me and many mamas through the mountains and valleys of motherhood and give us hope. By no means are these Scriptures to be considered the end-all conversation, but they are a good start. God has much more to say to the mama's heart; there are many more Scriptures in His Word and many more truths to be gleaned in direct and personal connection with Him. My prayer is that by the end of this devotional you see more of the ways that God calls you His beloved daughter and know that He has an invested relationship with you every minute of your life. He is your true Source in your mama journey. We can trust our mama's heart to God because He creates that heart within us and He takes care of us.

One morning on the way to school, while discussing what this devotional should be named with my kids, my youngest daughter, Alexa, added the phrase "to heal a mama's heart." She said (without knowing what any of the verses were) that the verses within this devotional "heal a mama's heart." Alexa continued, "Mom, there are too many women hurting and struggling. They don't believe they are good moms, but they *are* good moms. They need to know what God says about them. They need God to heal them." Tears came to my eyes when she spoke. These words were beyond her current scope of understanding of what a mom experiences in the mama journey.

God used my daughter's words and voice to speak truth to me and show me His love for mamas. At nine years old, she conveyed what mamas need. She knew that our internal struggle as both physical and spiritual moms is to know that God heals us and we are whole, complete, and lack nothing needed to help someone else. We need to know that in God we are enough and God shapes, forms, and equips us for the beautiful work of being a mama. Because He loves, we love. Because He is, we are.

Our mama's heart is where God speaks to moms. The mama's heart is the place within a woman that allows her to receive from God all that she needs to do the work He called for her to do within the family He gives. God has a lot to say to us that heals our mama's heart. However, what God says is often the opposite of what the world says. The world is not very nice to mamas and we are often mean to ourselves. The judgment, condemnation, and comparison traps we frequently default to are designed to derail our identity as daughters of God and undermine God's work in us as mamas.

God speaks to our mama's heart so that we know that our identity is secure in Him. The enemy's agenda is to steal, kill, and destroy (John 10:10) within the mama's heart. He attacks both a mom's identity as a beloved daughter and her relationship with God and says she has no purpose in Christ, disrupting the reception of what God has for her. But God's love for the mama's heart tells a different story. He secures our identity as beloved daughters, always keeps the relationship open, and gives us an unquestionable purpose in His kingdom.

My prayer is that as you read and work through this devotional you will know the comfort and safety of the Father's heart. I want you to find rest in His arms and realize more of God's presence in your life. The relationship God has with moms is real, tangible, and profound. God is alive and present in our everyday lives.

He designed us with a purpose like no other and, before our children were born—like He did for *us* in *our* mother's wombs—God spoke to our children and prepared us and them for an incredible adventure. If you are a biological mama, God utilized your physical womb and whispered deep conversations to your child. If you are an adopted mama, then God wove a special tale to your child and threaded that story to you. For the spiritual mama who loves, mentors, and relationally adopts children not her own, the mama's heart is powerfully strong in you, too. God has a plan for moms, and He made and loves the mama's heart. May these 30 verses heal your mama's heart and reveal more of who God created you to be.

You may have started and hopefully finished a plethora of devotionals before. However, since this is my first devotional, I want to share how to progress through this devotional study. If this is your first time working through a devotional, welcome! Dive in. You are among friends.

This devotional is designed to be more than a fifteen-minute pause to read some nice words and then go about your life. This *30 Verses to Heal a Mama's Heart* devotional is written to take your awareness of who you are in Christ to the next level as you engage your mama's heart with God. How long you take each day to read and process each devotion is up to you. I wrote this devotional as a one-month study. Some mamas may need more time to process each verse with God. That is okay. Take the time you need.

As you read each verse, I highly encourage you to commit that verse to memory. I memorize Scripture best by writing out the verse on notecards and then I read and repeat that verse frequently as I wait in the activities of my day. Do what works best for you to memorize the verses. Memorizing Scripture is important. We are told in the Bible that God's Word is alive (Hebrews 4:12). The more we memorize His words, the better we hear God's voice. Trust that God has something for you as you commit to seek Him more.

Included in every *Reflect and Receive* section are questions designed to help you seek the Father's heart. These questions are best asked and answered in a quiet environment. God always speaks to us, and He is better heard when our lives are less loud or distracting. Shut off your phone, turn off the TV, wake up early or stay up late; do whatever you need to do to have a few moments of silence. I'm a mom also. I know how premium silence can be. Silence is difficult for us to obtain but never impossible. Ask God to help you and provide a time and place to be still and listen to Him. He is eager to have time with you. I know silence can be awkward and uncomfortable at first. Let God teach you how to play the silence and become comfortable in stillness. It took me two years to learn to love and not rush the silence. I am certain you are a better student of stillness and silence than I was.

When you are first learning the discipline of stillness it may be easier to have silence. I don't need silence now to have stillness. I experience stillness in some noisy and chaotic places now, but that is a whole other story and another book. For now, silence and stillness likely will need to be paired for you. Stillness has become the ultimate atmosphere for me to know my Father's heart and experience His embrace. In stillness, we experience who God is and we receive physical, emotional, and mental rest. Every mama can benefit from this rest. My prayer is that God guides you to this sweet, restful presence with Him. Experiencing God's presence is a process, and the more you seek this restful place, the more you find it.

My desire as the facilitator of this devotional is that you grow comfortable with asking God questions about you. Expect that He has answers He wants to share with you. He made you. He loves you. He will talk to you. When God talks, He speaks words of life. If what you hear is not life-giving, what you are hearing is not God. God doesn't use anger, shame, or manipulation to draw us closer to Him. We are told in Romans 2:4 that God's goodness—His kindness—leads us to repentance. Reject any response that is not life-giving as "not God" and listen for God

Your responses to the *Reflect and Receive* questions are important. Write or draw your responses in your book. The answers God gives you serve as the way God tells you who He is and who you are. God heals you in His Father-daughter conversation with you. He divides your responsibility to receive from His responsibility to provide. You will find that as God does what God does, there is less for you to *do* and more for you to *be*. *Being* instead of *doing* seems easy, but receiving and *not* doing is more difficult for us than we often care to admit.

If you are reading this devotional, then likely you are here for answers. Your mama's heart probably hurts and feels bruised, wounded, or broken. I'm glad you are here. I wish I could give you a hug beyond these words. You are why I wrote this devotional. However, there is no way I or any other author can give you all the answers. That is God's role in your life. There is simply no book for mamas that is big enough or comprehensive enough to allow a mama to scan through an index, turn to a page, read a few words, and answer a few questions, and find every wound of their mama's heart—from toddler fits to teenager rebellion—healed. I would steer clear from any author that promises that. Instead, this devotional is a journey for you and me to walk through together to receive God's love and learn more about who we are and who He is.

As you pray the *Prayers* from each devotional, know that every prayer is prayed in Jesus's name whether that phrase is emphasized or not. Because of what Christ did for us, we can boldly communicate with God; *all* we do is in Jesus's name and by the power and authority given to us through Christ.

Remember that half the fun is the journey there. This devotional is designed to start a lifelong conversation with God who is connected to you. You are His beloved child, and you are on an incredible journey.

Much love,

Wendy M. Hamilton

Identity

Verse 1

The lines have fallen to me in pleasant places; Yes, I have a

good inheritance. (Psalm 16:6)

Beloved Daughter on an Incredible Journey

Before we can understand how God heals the mama's heart, we need to know who we are. We are not simply our parents' daughters; we are daughters of the King of kings and Lord of lords. We are God's daughters. As His daughters, there is a boundary line around us that is there to protect our daughter identity and lead us on the path God designed for us to travel. Our true Father knows who we are and what we are created to be.

The boundary lines He places around us are for our protection. As each of us were formed in our mother's womb, God whispered, "You are my beloved daughter." As He knit our form, our beings—who we would be, how we would laugh, the ways we would love, and everything that brings us joy and purpose—He gave us our boundary lines. He made us and called us "good" (Genesis 1:31).

Inside of those boundary lines is every gift and treasure God designed for us to have with His blessing and favor. We are safe and secure within what God gives us. Outside of those boundary lines, as we attempt to claim what was never ours, we only know fear and insecurity. In that out-of-bounds place, we become hurt, wounded, and broken. Our mama's heart becomes overwhelmed and damaged. We forget who we were created to be. We forget that we are beloved daughters of God.

God knew we would step outside of the boundaries. We are His beloved girls. He created that fierce will strong within each of us. He knew. And He made a way for us to rest in Him, return to the place He designed for us, and receive His perfect peace and love.

In this place, we are God's girls. No other title, degree, or accolade matters or is necessary. We are His. Here we know as we are known, and here in the Father's heart is the foundation for every good thing God determined would be ours. Here we have an incredible love and we are beloved.

Let God whisper to you that you are His beloved daughter. He has amazing plans for you and an adventure Divinely designed with you in mind.

GOD HAS AMAZING

PLANS FOR YOU

AND AN ADVENTURE

DIVINELY DESIGNED

WITH YOU

IN MIND.

Reflect and Receive

Ask God to show you how He created you and formed you in your mother's womb. Listen to God's words and write out what He said when He created you.

_____

_____

_____

_____

_____

_____

_____

_____

_____

_____

_____

_____

_____

_____

_____

_____

_____

_____

Psalm 139:17 claims, "How precious also are Your thoughts to me, O God! How great is the sum of them!" Think of how God tenderly and purposefully crafted who you are, and how He has the most precious thoughts about you, to you, and for you. Ask God to give you *one word* to help you know who you are. Write that *one word* below.

_____

Shame is not a tool of God but the way the enemy deceives you to step from the protective boundary lines God gave you. God gave you a beautiful inheritance in Him. Ask Him what that inheritance is.

_____

_____

_____

_____

_____

_____

_____

_____

_____

_____

_____

Prayer

God, help me to see how I am a beloved daughter of the King and Your words are life to me. If there is a difference between my definition of "father" and the true Father *you* are, I ask You to reveal to me how Your love and what Christ did for me on the cross covers that gap. You are my perfect Father. I rest in the knowledge of who You are. I am known to you. I am loved by you. I am Yours. Show me how to celebrate who I am in You. In Jesus's name. Amen.

Verse 2

Therefore, if anyone is in Christ, *she* is a new creation; old things have passed away; behold, all things have become new. (2 Corinthians 5:17, emphasis added)

New Creation in Christ

Your past does not define you. Who you were, the things you did or didn't do, or what you said or didn't say are not you. Those actions have no power to say who you are. As a beloved daughter of Christ, you have a new identity. This identity is one you received *first* when God created you, and *second*, when you were saved. You only need to receive what God did for you.

Our salvation occurred at the time Jesus Christ died on the cross for the full payment of our sins. More than 2000 years ago, Jesus Christ, God's Son, died for us so that we can be reconnected to God, our Source. We receive His salvation and live free as God's daughters. We receive the salvation Christ died to give us when we confess who Christ is and declare that what Christ did was *enough* to pay the full penalty of sin. Our connection to God that was severed by sin is reconnected fully through Christ.

What Christ did was complete. His actions forever changed the way God views you and communicates with you. Before Christ, all the wrong that was done required a sacrifice offered for that sin to be forgiven. Before Christ, when sin was forgiven, there were a few fleeting moments of connection with God before another sin was committed and the need for another sacrifice returned. Because Christ is our sacrifice, we have freedom now. There is no point for another sacrifice to be made. What Christ did was enough.

The salvation we receive through Christ is *powerful*. Christ's salvation is enough to take everything we were (the old us) and give us a new way of being (the new us). The old us can do no right. The new us *is* righteousness, or made right in Christ. There is absolutely nothing that we can do to undo what Christ did.

All our sins were paid for more than 2000 years before we sinned. However, knowing our sin is paid for and that we don't have to pay the spiritual penalty of sin does not mean that we continue to sin intentionally. In Christ, we know that the spiritual penalty of sin is paid for. What Christ did *for* us removed our sin *from* us and reconnected us to our Source: God. King David understood this, saying, "As far as the east is from the west, so far has He removed our transgressions from us (Psalm 103:12).

When God looks at us, His beloved daughters, He can't see our sin because what Christ did for us on the cross removed our sin. We are told in Hebrews 8:12 that God remembers our sins and our lawless deeds no more. God does not remember who we were. He only sees and defines us as the beloved daughters we are.

We are new creations in Christ; old things are passed away and everything is new (2 Corinthians 5:17).

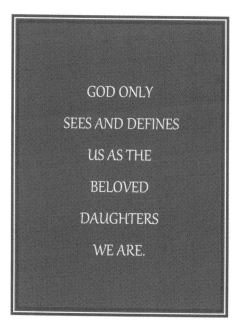

GOD ONLY

SEES AND DEFINES

US AS THE

BELOVED

DAUGHTERS

WE ARE.

Reflect and Receive

Ask God to reveal any sins—things you did or didn't do, said or didn't say—that you believe may be separating you from Him. Write what God showed you.

_____

_____

_____

_____

_____

_____

_____

_____

_____

_____

_____

_____

_____

_____

_____

_____

Now, write: **"Christ died for *all* my sins"** over your list. "Nothing separates me from God's love for me" (Romans 8:38–39).

Ask God to show you when you accepted His gift of salvation. If you do not recall a time where you acknowledged what Christ did for you on the cross and how His sacrifice is the complete payment of your sins, do that now.

Romans 10:8b–10 says, "The word is near you, in your mouth and in your heart" (that is, the word of faith which we preach): that if you confess with your mouth the Lord Jesus and believe in your heart that God has raised Him from the dead, you will be saved. For with the heart one believes unto righteousness, and with the mouth confession is made unto salvation."

Write your confession of your faith. This is your salvation story to share with someone else!

_____

_____

_____

_____

_____

_____

_____

_____

_____

_____

_____

_____

_____

_____

_____
_____
_____
_____
_____
_____
_____
_____
_____
_____
_____
_____
_____
_____
_____
_____
_____
_____
_____
_____
_____
_____
_____
_____

Prayer

God, all I ask You is through your Son's name. As I begin a renewed walk with You, show me who You are. Give me opportunities to reflect on what Christ did for me and what You do through me. Thank you, God, for the many ways You breathe life into me. You, God, give me strength. You are my focus as I become more of who You created me to be. God, if there is any woman who believes she is not worthy of Your love and Your grace, show her that the gift of Christ is hers to freely receive and that you freely give it to her. Remove any barrier or lie between me and Your perfect love. In Jesus's name. Amen

Verse 3

I can do all things through Christ

who strengthens me. (Philippians 4:13)

You Are Braver Than You Believe

As I wrote "You are braver than you believe," tears came to my eyes—not simply because it reminded me of earlier days in my children's lives when we would watch Winnie the Pooh and I'd hear their sweet, sing-song voices repeat Christopher Robin's words to the Pooh, "Promise me you'll always remember: You're braver than you believe, and stronger than you seem, and smarter than you think."[1] My tears came from a deeper place and a harder truth. I have tears because there is a real part of my mama's heart that wants to be braver than I believe I am.

Pay attention to what makes you cry. Your tears reveal a deeper truth. We don't cry at everything, only in response to truths that resonate deeply within our souls. I well up when I see the words, "You are braver than you believe" because writing is difficult for me. I did not believe for many years that I was brave enough to be a writer. I—the writer—have no clue if you—the reader—will like what I write. I have no idea if my words will convey the truths of God I am passionate about showing to you. I have rewritten more than 200 devotionals to get these thirty devotionals for this book; I know that I held nothing back. There is a part of me that God still speaks to, reminding me that His strength activated within me is enough. He tells me again and again, "Trust me. Write." In complete transparency, I often feel I am not brave enough to be me, and I bet there are days where you feel that you are not brave enough to be you.

God knows how difficult it is to be a mama. He knew before we became moms that our kids would love us one day and the next we'd be the "worst mom ever." He knew that we would need to know that His love never changes. He knew how empty our homes, days, and routines would seem when our child left for school for

---

[1] Pooh's Grand Adventure: The Search for Christopher Robin

her first day of kindergarten. He knew our mixed emotions of joy and dread when our child packed up his mountains of stuff to head off to college. He knew what we would experience and feel with our mama's heart as we loved our prodigal child. He gave us that love and told us that "My grace is sufficient for you, for My strength is made perfect in weakness" (2 Corinthians 12:9).

In those transitional moments when we don't feel brave enough, God remains true to His promise that He will never leave us or forsake us (Hebrews 13:5). He didn't leave us, He doesn't, and He won't ever. His presence in our life is an absolute, a done deal. God declared that He is the one that gives us strength. He tells us that He is at work in us to do good things. He declares that He will do more than we could ask or think. We are braver than we believe because God believes in us and He is always at work within us.

Through Christ, we have the strength to be brave and do all the things God called us to do, especially the hard, soul-squishing things. God is our strength. God at work in us accomplishes what we need, not of our doing, but by God doing. We receive and have all we need to be who we are supposed to be. Through Christ we can do all things because God strengthens us (Philippians 4:13).

Reflect and Receive

God loves us and He gave us our ability to feel deeply and trust Him completely. Ask God to show you where you need to trust Him more.

_____

_____

_____

_____

_____

_____

_____

_____

_____

_____

_____

_____

_____

_____

_____

_____

_____

_____

_____

Ask God if there is a place where you are relying more on your strength than His strength.

_____

_____

_____

_____

_____

_____

_____

_____

_____

_____

_____

_____

_____

_____

_____

_____

God fiercely invests in the mama's heart. Life happens in a mama's heart. Talk to God about anywhere your mama's heart hurts—for dreams, for your kids, for your spouse—and share with God where you believe you are not brave enough. Ask God to show you how He makes you brave, not of your doing, but by His power at work in your life.

_____

_____

_____

_____

_____

_____

_____

_____

_____

_____

_____

_____

_____

_____

_____

_____

_____

_____

_____

_____

Prayer

God, wow! Being a mama and stewarding this mama's heart can hurt. You created such an incredible journey for me as a mama and You have given me many opportunities to see You active, alive, and at work in what I perceive as good or bad. No matter what, You are God and You are my strength. God, thank You for the breath You breathe into me. You are my life. Let me take in all that You are and know Your strength in my everyday life. Thank You for the answers You give to my questions. You are all I need. In Jesus's name. Amen.

Verse 4

Before I formed you in the womb I knew you;

Before you were born I sanctified you; I ordained you a

prophet to the nations. (Jeremiah 1:5)

God Loves Me

Originally this devotional's title was *God Loves the Former Perfectionist, Trophy-Chaser Me*. However, I thought I would be nice to my editor, Karen, by simplifying the title and instead bringing that thought into the text. Here's the deal; you know who you are and I know who I am. For the most part I know my strengths and weaknesses and you know yours. There may be a few things we will figure out as we go along, but for the most part, the person that we are right now, we know. We already know what God wants us to know. For example, after I wrapped up writing that last devotional I looked at my husband, Mike, and confessed, "If I don't lighten up, I am going to drown my reader."

See, I understand myself. You can thank me later for the content I edited out and for how God pulled the reigns to bring us back to the surface, air, and sunlight. There is a time to delve into deep, thoughtful, and emotional places (and I am *good* at getting there!) and there is a time to rejoice at who God made us to be—imperfections and all!

I know that I can be awkward. I know that I'm the one on the greeter team at my church that has no idea what to do with my hands while I am standing there in between saying hello, giving hugs, waving, and welcoming people. I realize that I fidget when I'm nervous. I know that I have the sense of humor of an 5th grade boy and I can laugh at the most inopportune times when that humor kicks in. But despite all I know that is not primped and polished about me, I know that I love people. I love their uniqueness and quirkiness. I love how people smile differently, laugh differently, and speak differently. I love the varying colors people wear and the way they accessorize their everyday lives. Just as I know me, I know there is a unique blend of likes, dislikes, preferences, personality, dreams, and desires that make you who you are. God really did a good work.

When He formed you, He put good stuff into you, breathed life within you, and spoke wonderful words over you. In God, you and I become living souls. We become alive. God set us apart from every other person and every bit of creation. He designed us uniquely to be His own special version of ourselves. He made no mistake. He offsets our weaknesses with His strengths. He is with us, no matter how, who, what, where, when, or why. God knows we have questions and is excited with who He created us to be. God loves us.

Reflect and Receive

God is a Daddy rejoicing over His daughters. Jeremiah 1:5 shows us the intentional investment and design of God in our creation and Zephaniah 3:17 captures the joy God has for who we are.

The LORD your God in your midst,
The Mighty One, will save;
He will rejoice over you with gladness,
He will quiet *you* with His love,
He will rejoice over you with singing.

Ask God to show you where He is in the middle of all that you are.

_____

_____

_____

_____

_____

_____

_____

_____

Ask God how He saves you in your daily life.

_____

_____

_____

_____

_____

_____

_____

_____

_____

_____

_____

_____

_____

_____

_____

_____

_____

_____

_____

_____

_____

_____

_____

_____

_____

_____

Ask God how He rejoices over you with gladness and how He quiets you with His love.

_____

_____

_____

_____

_____

_____

_____

_____

_____

_____

God sings a song over you. The song God sings over you is celebratory and rejoicing. Ask God to tell you what that song is and write the words, thoughts, or emotions He gives below.

_____   _____
_____   _____
_____   _____
_____   _____
_____   _____
_____   _____
_____   _____
_____   _____
_____   _____
_____   _____
_____   _____
_____   _____
_____   _____
_____   _____
_____   _____
_____   _____
_____   _____
_____   _____

Prayer

God, You make me smile. You know how to bring Your joy to me. I am in awe of the way You celebrate me and all mamas. You sing over my mama's heart and rejoice over me. Thank You for the details You invested in each of Your beloved daughters, including me. Thank You that the words You speak over me are life, praise, and gratitude. You are my Source. You are my everything. You are all I need. I love You and am grateful for how You love me. In Jesus's name. Amen.

Verse 5

So God created man in His own image; in the image of God

He created him; male and female He created them.

(Genesis 1:27)

God Fixes Our Image Problem

While my daughter is away at college, I am the proud adopted mom of three bearded dragons—Drake, Maggie, and Baby. These bearded dragons, in addition to eating fruit and veggies from my garden, consume crickets. If you have no experience with creatures that are not dogs or cats, I'm so sorry for the knowledge that sweet chirpy crickets are being fed to those lizard-y things. For the rest of you, you know the food options could get a lot worse.

Recently I went shopping at my local pet store to buy crickets. Instead of the cheerful, bubbly, engaging gals and guys that usually helped me, I had *him. He* did absolutely nothing wrong and paid perfect attention to detail and retrieved the 150 large crickets I asked for. In fact, if I were his boss I would love him and give him a raise. However, unlike my other cricket acquirers who scooped and dumped while chatting and had my more than 150 crickets bagged and tagged in record time, he was methodically slow. I watched as he slowly counted each cricket as it jumped into the bag. One, two, three...I stared in impatient disbelief. *Are you kidding me?* The more I watched him the slower the cricket counting seemed to progress. Finally, he finished gathering my crickets, carefully wrote the quantity on the bag, and handed the bag of crickets to me. There were far fewer crickets than I usually received. "Are you sure there are 150 crickets in here?" I asked. "There are 157 crickets," he smiled warmly, "I gave you are few extra in case a couple die." What could I do except tell him thank you? The problem wasn't with him but with my expectation; I had a preconceived image of what cricket-buying should be like.

As I reflected on that experience I thought of how we often have similar image problems in our expectations of ourselves and God. God tells us we are made in His image, yet we want to focus on all our flaws. He says that He wants to have a relationship with us but we want to argue with Him and tell Him that He really doesn't and we aren't good company. God tells us we have a purpose and we still question the same. At some point, we need to reset the conversation (now is a good time) and say, "So, God created me in His image. In the image of God, I am created," and let that truth shape who we are. We need to add on a bit of detail from Genesis 1:28 where God gave us a purpose: to be fruitful and multiply, to fill the earth and to subdue it. We might also want to add that in Genesis 1:31, when God surveyed all the He created, He said what He created was "very good." Not merely good—God said what He created was *very* good. Our Father God, our Creator, the One who created us describes us, with all our quirks, differences, and weaknesses as very good.

When we think about ourselves and describe who we are, our words should reflect His. God's words fix our image problem. His words create and bring life where there is little or no life. When our words match God's words, we share in creation and we bring life no matter who or what we encounter.

Reflect and Receive

You are created in the image of God. If your image of God is good, then how you define yourself is a good thing. If your image of God is smudged by your experiences, then you need better definitions of who God is. Ask God to reset your definitions of who He is. Ask Him for a renewed view of who He is and write out the words God gives to describe Himself.

_____

_____

_____

_____

_____

_____

_____

_____

_____

_____

_____

_____

_____

_____

_____

_____

_____

As a beloved daughter created in the image of God, as He is, so you are. Ask God to tell you more about who you are and to speak life into your identity as His beloved daughter.

_____

_____

_____

_____

_____

_____

_____

_____

_____

_____

_____

_____

_____

_____

_____

_____

_____

_____

_____

_____

Prayer

God, thank You for all You bring to my everyday life. You promised that Your mercies renew each morning and I am grateful for how You reset my life. God, thank You for the many ways You draw me close and tell me that I am Your beloved daughter. Help me understand more of who You are. In Jesus's name. Amen

.

Verse 6

The end of a thing *is* better than its beginning; The patient

in spirit *is* better than the proud in spirit.

(Ecclesiastes 7:8)

God Knows Us

When I was a young girl trying to decide if I wanted to read a book or not, I would read the first three pages, two pages somewhere in the middle of the book, and the final five pages. If I felt the author resolved the story well I would read the book. I realize this sounds insane because as I read I knew the ending. However, my parents limited the number of books I could check out of the library each week and I wanted to be sure that each book was a good investment of my time. I had no desire to reach the end of the book and feel disappointed.

What worked well for me to select books doesn't work for my mama's heart. The events and circumstances that hurt my mama's heart never have a clear ending that I can fast forward to and review to see if the resolution works. I can't see the end to determine if I want to experience that event or circumstance. Practical wisdom tells me that I do not have the privilege of knowing the end of the matter before I experience the beginning and walk through the middle. My participation is not optional.

We are not fans of not knowing. We are uncomfortable with discomfort. We are wired to ask why, and we want answers—and the sooner the better. We do not like the ache of not knowing, even though in that in-between place we are known fully by God. God knows our needs. God whispers, "Do you trust me?" and we often answer, "I'm not sure." God continues to walk with us and talk to us in every step between the beginning and the end. He doesn't require our trust before He is faithful. He is faithful no matter what. God knows us. He knows that that more we realize who He is and that He isn't going anywhere, we will grow to trust Him more. God is faithful and His answers are good. The more we learn about Him the more we don't need to know what we don't know. We don't need to know how everything works out for our mama's heart to know that God holds us in the storm. We don't need to know the details of every step in-between; we only need to know that God is with us individually and personally in this present step. We don't need to know the end to know that God will bring us through the middle just as He brings us through every beginning. We can trust who God is even when we don't know.

God teaches our mama's heart that we don't need to stare at reasons and deduce answers. We can trust Him and follow. We don't have to hunger and search for the reason why. God is all we need in every situation. He provides. He moves. He gives. We receive.

The love within the Father's heart is what connects our mama's heart to His. He is our Source. He is our solution. As we seek God, He calms our worries and what ifs. He gives us an incredible amount of grace and mercy which becomes our sustaining strength from beginning to end.

Reflect and Receive

God will settle your mama's heart in every storm. He will give you peace as you patiently wait and trust Him. His Spirit at work in your life yields better results than your prideful spirit. God at work within you provides all you need to wait on Him and not rush ahead in your own strength. Ask God if there is an area of your mama's heart where you are uncomfortable with waiting on Him or need to trust Him more.

_____

_____

_____

_____

_____

_____

_____

_____

_____

_____

_____

_____

God's timing is perfect. Think about a time where you waited and what God did in your situation was more than you imagined.

_____

_____

_____

_____

_____

_____

_____

_____

_____

_____

_____

_____

_____

_____

_____

_____

_____

_____

_____

_____

_____

_____

God's words to you in the between moments are always life. If there have been words spoken by you or to you in a situation that weren't words of life or life-giving, ask God to give you different words that offer you hope, peace, and comfort, and show God's faithfulness and love to you. Write those new words below.

_____

_____

_____

_____

_____

_____

_____

_____

_____

_____

_____

_____

_____

Prayer

God, You are the One who frees me from bad definitions. The words You speak over me are life. Thank You for the abundance of words You give me that show me again and again that You are faithful. Thank You for loving me despite the many times I am slow to trust who You say You are. You have declared yourself to be my Provider, my Hope, my Salvation, my Friend, my Deliverer, my Comfort, my Rock, my Tower, and more. You are my Safe Place. God, I am so incredibly grateful for the ways You protect my mama's heart. You allow nothing to sever the link and connection between You. Because I am Your daughter, You allow me to come boldly to Your throne and You listen to me. You hear my cries and You are all I need. I love you. Thank You, God for who You are. In Jesus's name. Amen

.

Verse 7

Love has been perfected among us in this:

that we may have boldness in the day of judgment;

because as He is, so are we in this world. (1 John 4:17)

Who God Says

To understand our identity, we need to better understand who God is. 1 John 4:17 reminds us that "Because as He is, so are we in this world." The god that is known, talked about, criticized, and hated in our world is not God. God doesn't hate us, send hurricanes to chase us down and tell us repent or else. God is love perfected. Said another way, He never does anything wrong in His love for us and His love is exactly what we need. His kindness leads us to repentance.

The god misrepresented in the words and actions of those who don't know Him and within the hearts and lives of many who claim they *do* know Him, is not God. We can't make God speak for us, nor can we speak anything falsely about God. What defines God as God is not affected by what we say or don't say, or do or don't do. Who God is sticks and stays through time.

God represents and operates in the fruit of the Spirit: love, joy, peace, longsuffering, kindness, goodness, faithfulness, gentleness, and self-control. Everything God is cannot operate in an opposing spirit to the Spirit of God whose fruit is love, joy, peace, longsuffering, kindness, goodness, faithfulness, gentleness, and self-control. God does not do what is not God. God does not say what is not God. Jesus, God in human form, called Himself Light (John 8:12), the Way, the Truth, and the Life (John 14:6) and He is same yesterday, today, and forever (Hebrews 13:8).

God frees us from all that is not Him. If what is called God goes against who He is, we can reject that as not-God. Anything not-God is not God. God is. Because God is who He is, He removes the responsibility of striving and achieving from us. We don't have to do anything to receive who He is at work in us and through us. We receive. His love is already perfected, whole, and complete, and requires nothing from us other than our willingness to receive.

57

Because He is, we have boldness and confidence in our everyday life. Because He is, we have the fruit of the Spirit in our mama's heart. We have unrestricted access to love, joy, peace, longsuffering, kindness, goodness, faithfulness, gentleness, and self-control. We have all we need to be the daughters He created us to be. Because He is, we are.

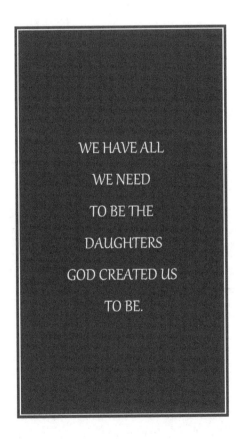

WE HAVE ALL

WE NEED

TO BE THE

DAUGHTERS

GOD CREATED US

TO BE.

Reflect and Receive

The world has much to say about God that is not God. Ask God to show you if there is anything or anyone in your world that is claiming to represent God but is not.

_____

_____

_____

_____

_____

_____

_____

_____

_____

_____

_____

_____

_____

_____

_____

_____

_____

_____

_____

There are many who claim to know God but represent attributes, traits, and an opposing spirit to God. Ask God to identify any thoughts or actions in your life or with those who claim to know God that may sound good, but are not God.

_____

_____

_____

_____

_____

_____

_____

_____

_____

_____

_____

_____

_____

_____

_____

_____

God wants you to know and explore who He is so you can better know who you are. You are made in His image and because of His perfected love you have the fruit of the Spirit and all God is operating within you as a gift from Him that you can give to others. Ask God to show you what you freely receive from Him that you can freely give to others.

_____

_____

_____

_____

_____

_____

_____

_____

_____

_____

_____

_____

_____

_____

_____

_____

_____

_____

_____

Prayer

God, thank You for the many ways You reveal the fruit of the Spirit in my life. I am grateful for how You give to me the treasure of who You are and how You allow me to freely give that gift to others. God, help me to be open to seeing You alive and at work in my everyday life. Allow my mama heart to rest in the complete love You give me and that Jesus provided for me in His name. In Jesus's name. Amen.

Verse 8

And you shall know the truth, and the truth shall make you free. (John 8:32)

Truth Will Set You Free

All God is and all He says we are is the truth designed to set us free. When God originally created us, His design was for us to be completely connected to Him and have a relationship with Him. God designed us in His image (Genesis 1:27) and desired for us to be His children (1 John 3:1). When Adam chose to disobey God, Adam's choice severed the connection between God and Adam and between God and us. Adam's choice disrupted the purpose God blessed us with to be fruitful, multiply, and subdue the earth (Genesis 1:28). The relational tool we received from God to bring chaos into order was disconnected by one man's choice. Adam's choice brought sin and spiritual death from sin to himself and to all of us because all of us have sinned (Romans 5:12). Spiritually we died when Adam sinned and our connection to God, our Source, was broken.

The remedy for sin and death is Christ. What Christ did for us on the cross completely reset our state and standing before God. We, who could only know sin and therefore sin, were saved by Jesus who God "made Him who knew no sin to be sin for us, that we might become the righteousness of God in Him" (2 Corinthians 5:21).

God loved us—His creation, created in His image—so much that He gave His Son, Jesus, to take all the sin, death, and separation upon Himself so that we could return to who we were created to be. Our identity comes not from what we do but what Christ did. Christ paid the price so we could be free.

You are not an afterthought; you are His *first* thought. God wanted you. The connection and relationship He created for us to have with Him is completely reconnected in Christ. The link between you and God is at 100 percent, with perfect reception. God hears your cries.

God speaks and you receive. God loves and you receive. Every good gift from God is yours not because of what you have done or do, but because of what God did for you, Christ gave to you, and the Holy Spirit empowers within you. God, as Father, Son and Spirit, sees us as daughters created in His image. Each of us have His likeness and the ability to receive Christ and function in the fruit of the Spirit in our everyday lives. Everything God is works toward your redemption and freedom. God wants you and me to be free and He is the Truth that sets us free.

Reflect and Receive

Christ died to restore your connection with God. Because He is, you are. Your works and good deeds are not a requirement for God to love you and desire a relationship with you. Any deficit you have is undone by who God is. Ask God to show you any area where you believed you needed to work to earn your connection to Him.

_____

_____

_____

_____

_____

_____

_____

_____

_____

_____

_____

_____

_____

Thank God for the many ways He shows that He is connected to you. The power of sin is no more. You are alive in Christ and are a new creation through Him. Take time and celebrate your love and connection for who God is.

Think about God's blessing to you that provides all you need to be fruitful, multiply, and subdue the earth. Adam's sin separated you from this blessing, but Christ's sacrifice restored God's blessing to you. Ask God what He wants you to know about this blessing.

Prayer

God, You are Truth. No matter what is said against You, nothing changes who You are. Thank You for the many ways You pour Your love into my life. I am grateful for all that You are. Every day You show me who You are more and more. Thank You for the ways You speak and guide me and tell me that You are my strength. I trust in who You are. Help me learn more about You and give me the words to tell others about You. In Jesus's name. Amen.

Verse 9

Therefore, we were buried with Him through baptism into death, that just as Christ was raised from the dead by the glory of the Father, even so we also should walk in newness of life. (Romans 6:4)

By the Glory of the Father: Walk

Too often I can read a verse of Scripture with many big, powerful truths, and I gloss over the very words that could shatter the walls around my heart. The enemy distracts us from the truth of God's words. He has no desire that we rest in what God did for us. For example, in Romans 6:4, there is almost a clinical presentation of salvation—Christ was buried and raised. As I read, I almost feel Satan trying to whoosh me by the rest of the verse with a "nothing to see here" while he whispers, "so move on."

God held me still and settled me on one phrase: *by the glory of the Father. By the glory of the Father.* I read those words and let them break light upon my darkness. I let light flood the deep places of my heart and fill me and give me strength.

The enemy has no desire for you to hear that you are a beloved daughter and that God created you in His image and likeliness. The enemy will stop at nothing to push every trigger and button and activate any number of situations and circumstances around you to distract you. He lies to us and tell us that there is nothing to see when God says He is there and His glory is all around us. The very presence of God floods our aching mama's hearts and tells us that we are not alone and we are known. We might feel invisible here, but in the heart of the Father, we are fully known and fully loved. Heaven holds nothing good from us and satisfies our desires.

By the glory of the Father we walk. We walk boldly and with authority. We come as daughters of the King to stand in front of His throne and feel the Father's arms gather us close in the full protection of His never-ending love. We rest here in the Father's heart. Our closed-off hearts are unwalled. What was once barely beating within us becomes a new heart in Christ, awake, aware, and alive in a newness of life that we never knew before.

The presence of God fills us with joy, laughter, and strength, and gives us all we need to fulfill the Divine purpose God ignites within us. By the glory of the Father we are. By the glory of the Father we walk. We take next steps as God leads us and we know that every step we walk is walked with Him. The One who promises to never leave us or forsake us never will. His love is constant and contains us within the most beautiful boundary lines—the Father's heart. We walk from this place where our spirit connects with His Spirit. We know that from the place, we are known.

The glory of the Father does the impossible and defeats death in every form in our lives. By His glory, the Father calls us back to life, back to connection, and into relationship with Him. By the glory of the Father we walk in newness of life.

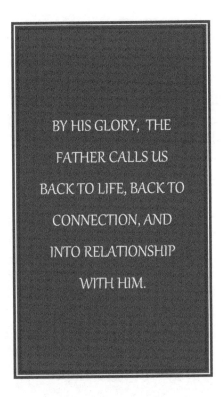

BY HIS GLORY, THE
FATHER CALLS US
BACK TO LIFE, BACK TO
CONNECTION, AND
INTO RELATIONSHIP
WITH HIM.

Reflect and Receive

God wants to know you and for you to know that by His glory you walk in newness of life. He gives you all you need to be the daughter you were created to be. Ask God to show you what He gives you to be the daughter He created you to be.

_____

_____

_____

_____

_____

_____

_____

_____

_____

_____

_____

_____

_____

_____

_____

_____

_____

_____

Your best connection starts in the Father's heart. Ask God to reveal the way He wants to be more in a relationship with you—focused not on what you do, but what He does.

_____

_____

_____

_____

_____

_____

_____

_____

_____

_____

_____

_____

_____

_____

_____

_____

_____

_____

_____

_____

_____

God knows you may often focus on the big things and miss His tiny whisper. Let God slow your life and day and reveal to you the many ways He wants to speak in unending conversation with you. Sometimes, relationship with Him will require that you exchange good for best. Ask God where you can make time and space to listen.

Monday:

Tuesday:

Wednesday:

Thursday:

Friday:

Saturday:

Sunday:

Prayer

God, You are my joy. You take my brokenness and make me whole. You take my questions and give me answers. You offset my weakness with Your strength. God, help me discover You more. Show me where I make excuses or let the things of this world and my life distract me from listening to You. God, if I am afraid of what You will say, speak to me and tell me how Your perfect love casts out my fear (1 John 4:18). I am yours and am beloved by You. Thank you, God. In Jesus's name. Amen.

Verse 10

I will take you as My people, and I will be your God. Then you shall know that I am the Lord your God who brings you out from under the burdens of the Egyptians. (Exodus 6:7)

The Greatest Exchange

We each have our own unique version of the burdens of Egypt. We have the routines, thoughts, and patterns that make us question everything God whispered to us in our mother's wombs. We have enough sorrow and predictable responses to make us wonder if there truly are going to be good things happening for us and the family God gave to us. Our worlds close in on our mama's heart so fiercely at times that we are not sure if we are truly alive and living. Too often our thoughts are, "Surely, there is more to life than this."

It is in this broken place, where our mama's heart cracks and we seem so fragile, that God speaks. With His words, He makes the greatest exchange. He turns our tears to laughter and trades our sorrow for His joy. He says who He is. He says who we are. He says who He will be. He says we will know. He says He brings us out from the burdens of our Egypt. He gives us rest. He brings us from captive thoughts to lands He promised to us. He gives His beloved daughters freedom in Him.

His love activates a deep Father-child connection we can feel. His love makes us want to run to Him. He is ready for our full embrace. His grace, He says, is enough. He promises His strength is made perfect in our weakness. He has waited for us. He watched for us. He drew us to Him. God takes us and unites us to Him in a declaration stronger than blood. He calls us His own. We are His people. You are God's person. You are His sweet girl. You are His daughter and all that your heart needs He fills within you. He hears your hungry songs and answers your cries with songs of His own. The refrains He sang over you in the past, He continues to sing— and sings more. What He sings are more than words; He sings life.

What Egypt meant to you is no more. Your Egypt is a burden God takes from you. He removes the burden from you and He carries you. You are not captive under the patterns, thoughts and routines of this world. God gives you new thoughts, new routines, and new patterns that are His own, and He transforms you in every way from an orphan in your Egypt to be His daughter in His presence.

You are His girl. You are His own and He is your God.

Reflect and Receive

God made your mama's heart a daughter's heart. Ask God what you need to know as His daughter.

_____

_____

_____

_____

_____

_____

_____

_____

_____

_____

_____

_____

_____

_____

_____

_____

_____

_____

You have a Divinely instilled need to belong; God created that desire within you. He declares that He made you, and He is your God. His design was always for you to be connected to Him and to others. He gave you, through Him, all you need to belong. Ask God to show you if there is an area in your life where you struggle to belong.

_____
_____
_____
_____
_____
_____
_____
_____
_____
_____
_____
_____
_____
_____
_____
_____
_____
_____
_____
_____

God longs to take your captive heart and set you free. He removes the burdens of Egypt—the weight you are under—from you. Ask God to show you any burdens of your Egypt that you carry and that He wants to remove from you.

_____

_____

_____

_____

_____

_____

_____

_____

_____

_____

_____

_____

_____

_____

_____

_____

_____

_____

Prayer

God, You remove the space between me and You. You place Your name upon me and call me Your own. I am yours. You are Emmanuel, God with me. You are my home. You place my lonely heart in Yours and You remove the burdens and cares of this world from me. There are no limits to your love and I am incredibly grateful for the many ways you transform my life. You take me from my Egypt and set me in Your kingdom. Nothing separates me from Your love. Nothing separates me from You, and I am grateful.

Relationship

Verse 11

And we know that all things work together for good to those who love God, to those who are the called according to His purpose. (Romans 8:28)

God at Work

Knowing that we are God's daughters is not everything that God wants us to know. God also wants us to know that no matter what happens in our lives, He will work all things together for good. This means the best moment of your life to every hurtful, tear-producing moment you encounter is what God will work together for good. God excludes nothing. He utilizes everything. That situation that feels like death is exactly what God will use to reveal His life. What feels like an awesome experience but isn't, or what we believe is the worst thing that can happen to us, all these things—the everything of our lives—are what God works together for our good.

God is at work in our everyday lives because He loves us. He loves us. God loves us with this crazy fierce, never-ending, hope-producing love that strengthens us. He is the only One who can love us like that. God can activate our spouses, our friends, and our kids to love us, but no one will be able to love us like God does. No one else can work together all things for good. Only God can do such good work according to His purpose. We can't do that. Each of us carry enough self-interest to derail good. You and I are simply not God.

God at work in our lives means that we might find ourselves in an uncomfortable season of waiting or receiving instead of doing. We are okay in this place. We rest in a posture of God-does instead of striving in a we-do mindset. We aren't God. We make mistakes and we don't know everything there is to know. Only God is infallible and omniscient. Only God knows all there is to know. What we can't see, God sees. What we don't know, God makes visible. God's relationship with us changes everything.

God uses the mama's heart to bring good. When God reveals good to us and works all things for good, He does what He does out of love for us—not because we do, but because He does. He is always at work in our lives to bring all things together for good.

GO IS ALWAYS AT

WORK IN OUR LIVES

TO BRING ALL THINGS

TOGETHER FOR GOOD.

Reflect and Receive

There is so much more stirring under the surface of your everyday life than what you know. God is alive and at work in your life, and He does not change. Who God was in the past is who He will be. Ask God where He was victorious in the past and where He brought good to your life.

God knows your limits. He does not need you to know everything or solve every problem. His relationship with you creates the environment for you to rest and receive. He is at work. Talk to God about a difficult situation you are experiencing and ask Him to show you how He causes all things to work together for good.

_____

_____

_____

_____

_____

_____

_____

_____

_____

_____

_____

_____

_____

_____

_____

_____

_____

_____

_____

_____

_____

Prayer

God, thank You for the ways You are alive and at work in my everyday life. You overcome all and You make all things work together for my good. In you, my stories are good. You are my Comfort, my Strength, and my Very Present Help. You are my Defender and my Protector. You are my Savior and You are my Friend. I trust in you. I trust in Jesus's name. Amen.

Verse 12

Peace I leave with you, My peace I give to you; not as the world gives do I give to you. Let not your heart be troubled, neither let it be afraid. (John 14:17)

God Gives Peace

The peace the world offers does not eliminate fear, nor does it free our mama's heart from troubled thoughts. The world says that as mamas the answers should come from us and the solutions must be ours. The world demands that we know how to make wrong things right and how to make right things happen immediately. True peace is nowhere to be found in the world's definition of peace. The peace the world gives is the best soil to grow worry, anxiety, fear, cares, and concerns.

God's peace, however, is different. His peace is relational, not distant, but with us and given to us. We have God's peace. We don't have to pray His peace to us. We don't have to will His peace to come to us. We don't have to do good for God to release it. God already gave us peace when He gave us Jesus who is our Peace. God already gave peace to us when He gave us the Holy Spirit to reside within us. What we need we already have in relationship to the Father's heart. Peace is ours to keep through the victory of Christ.

Because what we need is what we have, there is no need to be troubled. We don't have to be afraid. The presence of God in our lives changes everything. His peace passes our understanding and guards our mama's hearts and minds from all the world says is our responsibility. The world says, "Fix it," but God's peace says what is broken is not ours to fix. God's peace takes the world's definition of peace—a place without conflict—and tells us that what the world says is a partial truth. Peace is complete only through Christ by the power of the Holy Spirit within us. It is His peace that calms storms; sometimes He unravels storms outside of us, and other times, He unravels the storm within.

"My peace I give you" is God's Divine declarative telling us that no matter what we are never alone. Our God fights for us so we don't have to. Our God wins every battle, every time. We are champions

92

in Christ. We do not have to be afraid. We do not have to be troubled. We can choose to look to God in every situation. We can choose Him as our only answer. Who He is changes everything. We have peace in Him.

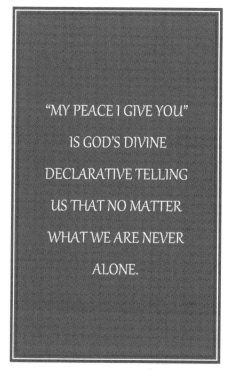

"MY PEACE I GIVE YOU" IS GOD'S DIVINE DECLARATIVE TELLING US THAT NO MATTER WHAT WE ARE NEVER ALONE.

Reflect and Receive

Peace and contentment go hand in hand. Perhaps God is teaching you to rest in Him. Who He is calms every storm. Talk to God about a current storm in your life that troubles you. Ask God what He wants to talk to you about regarding what you are experiencing.

_____

_____

_____

_____

_____

_____

_____

_____

_____

_____

_____

_____

_____

_____

_____

_____

_____

_____

The world's definition of a mama places the responsibility of your children's behavior on you. Who you are is often attached to what your children do or don't do, or say or don't say. God's definition of you, however, is greater and is independent of what your children do or say or who they are. His words heal the hurt from what others said you are. Ask God to speak to you about who you are and give you words to strengthen you in the storm.

_____

_____

_____

_____

_____

_____

_____

_____

_____

_____

_____

_____

_____

_____

_____

_____

_____

_____

God's peace provides rest. He longs to lift your burdens from you and give you the opportunity to rest in Him. Take a few minutes and rest quietly in the Father's heart. Humble yourself before Him, aware that He is your Source and He is your help. Cast all your care upon Him, for He cares for you (1 Peter 5:7).

_____

_____

_____

_____

_____

_____

_____

_____

_____

_____

_____

_____

_____

_____

_____

_____

_____

Prayer

Father God, You are a good Father. Thank You for never leaving me alone in the storm and for the many ways You calm my thoughts and relieve stress and tension from my mind. You are my answer and my Hope. You are the Prince of Peace and the Lord of lords. You are above the storm and I rest in the stillness within the Father's heart. I love You and am thankful for all that You are.

Verse 13

Every good gift and every perfect gift is from above, and comes down from the Father of lights, with whom there is no variation or shadow of turning. (James 1:17)

Source

When I was five years old, I found a stuffed dog in the store. The moment I picked up this dog I knew I wanted him. It was Christmas time, but nonetheless, I looked at my mom and pleaded, "Mom, can I have him?" Her eyes showed her dilemma—any toys purchased now should be a surprise. I stood in front of my mom and held the very item I wanted as a gift. "I've already bonded with it," I reasoned. I recall the ache in my heart as she said that she wouldn't purchase the dog at that time and that I needed to put him back on the shelf. What I didn't know then was that as my mom led me away from the toy section, my dad bought the dog for me. In my stack of presents on Christmas day, packaged some miraculous way inside of an egg carton, was the dog I desired, the toy I declared was perfect for me and that I longed for. My parents knew what I wanted and needed in that moment and they were my source of this perfect gift.

In that moment, they understood what I wanted and needed, and got it right. However, like every parent, including myself, there were moments where my parents missed the mark and gifts were not perfect or what I wanted or needed. As people disappoint and the gifts of their words and actions hurt us, God knows our mama's heart. He knows what we need and He tells us that He is our Provider. God provides for us consistently and constantly. He is our Source. Philippians 4:19 tells us that, "God shall supply all your need according to His riches in glory by Christ Jesus." The promise we have is that God supplies all of our needs. Every good and perfect gift comes from Him (James 1:17).

All that is not God is an inadequate source. No other part of creation can provide for us like God. The enemy likes nothing more than to twist and turn situations against us. What he gives is designed to steal, kill, and destroy (John 10:10). What God provides are good, perfect, and unchanging gifts.

The enemy questions the Source within us—he always has and always will. Conversely, God declares that His provision does not change. Our enemy grumbles and roars around us seeking to devour the fruit of the Spirit in our lives. But God fights for us ensuring that all that we need is provided. Nothing can separate us from His love. The enemy lies and tells us that we are the only one experiencing these feelings. God says that what we experience in life we have in common with others. He establishes Himself as the One with the unquestionable authority in our lives. He is our Source.

Reflect and Receive

God is your provision and Provider. He is what you need and everything comes from Him. Ask God to show you the ways He is your Source.

_____   _____

_____   _____

_____   _____

_____

_____

_____

_____   _____

_____   _____

_____   _____

GOD

IS MY

SOURCE.

There is nothing too trivial to God. The smallest details of your life is important to Him. Is there anything that you feel silly speaking to God about? Talk to Him. Share your heart with the One who gives good, perfect gifts and is unchanging.

_____

_____

_____

_____

_____

_____

_____

_____

_____

_____

_____

_____

_____

_____

_____

_____

_____

_____

_____

_____

_____

_____

Prayer

God, You tell me that Your grace is enough. You declare Your rightful place in my life as my Source. There is nothing that stands against You. Thank You, God, for the victory I have in Christ. God, thank You for listening to my heart. Every detail of who I am matters to You. Nothing goes unnoticed. You hear my cries and You answer my prayers. I am grateful for the gift You are.

Verse 14

He restores my soul; He leads me in the paths of righteousness For His name's sake. (Psalm 23:3)

God Restores

God, as Shepherd of our mama's hearts, ensures that we have what we need. We lack nothing under His care and provision. God restores our soul. That place within us that holds hurt and separates us situationally and relationally from others is where God speaks.

He knows that for us to have hearts of flesh instead of hearts of stone (Ezekiel 36:26) He must restore our souls. He changes what we know and expect to what He designed. He allows us to see others and see ourselves as children He loves no matter what. He gives us a new spirit within us and a new heart of flesh so that we connect to Him and receive, without interruption, from Him.

With a restored soul, we don't process life and people through filters of pain and past wounds. Instead, God teaches us to walk in paths of righteousness. He teaches us to process the world around us through His created design. He leads us to see others through redemptive eyes and see that just as Christ died to free us from sin and reconnect us to our true Source, Christ died to give that same gift to others.

Where God leads is motivated by God's good character, and for our salvation. The journey with Jesus and our walk with God saves us from ourselves and heals our wounds. The more we walk with God, the more we see His faithfulness in our lives. We know that what God does for us and the gifts He gives us are good. The more we know who God is, the more God softens our hearts.

All that God does is for His name's sake. He is who He is and He does what He says He will do. His nature cannot do anything else. God guides and leads us. He delivers us and keeps us from harm. He forgives us of our sin. The life He gives us is for His name's sake, for His glory. We are His own. We are His beloved daughters and He loves us. Because of His love for us, God won't let us hurt and suffer without His comfort. He cares for us and never leaves us.

Because of who God is, He restores your soul. He leads you in the paths of righteousness for His namesake—or what His name represents. God speaks to us as a shepherd cares for his sheep as Isaiah wrote: "Your ears shall hear a word behind you, saying, 'This is the way, walk in it,' Whenever you turn to the right hand Or whenever you turn to the left" (Isaiah 30:21).

We are never alone in this journey and God restores and leads us because of who He is and who we are.

Reflect and Receive

You may remember Psalm 23 from a funeral. This passage of Scripture is popular to read as a form of comfort to those grieving the loss of someone they knew and loved. God designed Psalm 23:3 and all the verses within Psalm 23 to inspire you in your everyday life. Read Psalm 23 and ask God to highlight His promises to you.

_____

_____

_____

_____

_____

_____

_____

_____

_____

_____

_____

_____

_____

_____

_____

_____

_____

_____

_____

Prayer

God, thank You for leading me so well. Show me more of what life is like resting in Your arms like a lamb in the arms of its shepherd. You care so completely for me. My heart trusts in You. God, there is nothing about me that You overlook. You tell me that You see my going out and my coming in—the details of my day are known by You, and You are in control. Thank You for the peace You give me and the love I know in You.

Verse 15

Take My yoke upon you and learn from Me, for I am gentle

and lowly in heart, and you will find rest for your souls.

(Matthew 11:29)

The Father's Rest

If your to-do list is anything like mine, as soon as you awake, what you "need" to do seems a little scary. Even consolidating and prioritizing my tasks to my Top 3 can feel a bit overwhelming. Recently my son asked me what I was thinking about. "You look stressed, Mom." I told him I was trying to figure out what I needed to do in the day. "Do you really need to or do you want to?" I stared at him, half frustrated that he was drilling down to the heart of the matter and half-excited that he presented the dilemma we deal with in our to-do lists every day. We confuse need to with want to.

Most of the items on our to-do lists are want-to not need-to items. We have flexibility. We do not have to function from a place of stress when there is a place of rest available. God instructs us to "take His yoke" upon us. Said another way, God asks His children to do what He asks—and what He asks is never too much. His way is designed to teach the posture and positioning of rest. In His presence, doing what He asks, we find rest.

God is relational. His Father-child relationship with us seeks to protect who we are. God restores our mama's hearts with His gentle and lowly methods. God is not pushy, but invitational. He invites us to experience life at different pace and in His perfect timing. What He offers us in this different-from-the-world place is the rest we need.

In busy, me-do mindsets I can miss the importance of this quiet, time of reflection with God. I can become so focused on the task that I forget that God designed me for connection and relationship with Him. He designed us to partner with Him and work side-by-side with Him, learning from Him how to live, move, and have our being in Christ (Acts 17:28).

God doesn't beat us up for not completing everything He asks. He is gentle and lowly in heart! His way is consoling and comforting. God is encouragement and strength.

Through His rest, He speaks.

THROUGH

HIS

REST,

HE

SPEAKS.

Reflect and Receive

God will never overburden you, His child. He invites you to take *His* yoke upon yourself—to work in partnership with Him. His yoke is easy and His burden is light. Ask God to show you if there are areas where you are overburdening your mama's heart.

_____

_____

_____

_____

_____

_____

_____

_____

_____

_____

God's way is a way of rest. He works for you and with you. God is waiting to partner with you to fulfill the purpose He has for you. The enemy will lie and tell you that you are alone and the work is up to you. Ask God to reveal these lies—where the enemy is telling you that you work alone.

_____
_____
_____
_____
_____
_____
_____
_____
_____
_____
_____
_____
_____
_____
_____
_____
_____
_____
_____
_____
_____
_____

God designed rest for your sake because you need rest. Make a list of what you "need to" accomplish in your day and ask God to show you the differences between "need to" and "want to." Then, ask Him where, when, and how He wants you to rest in Him.

Task	Need to	Want to

Prayer

God, You are my Rest. You are the place I can come to receive more of who You are. In Your presence, I receive every good gift I need. You are the Beginning and the End. You are everlasting. You are never-changing. In your Father's heart, I know I am loved beyond words and I am filled by Your love. God, thank You for who You are and the rest I receive from You. In Jesus's name. Amen.

Verse 16

And my God shall supply all your need according to His riches in glory by Christ Jesus. (Philippians 4:19)

Provider

Each of us has a button the enemy pushes. This trigger reveals a soul wound that God is healing and working out in our lives. My button is financial provision, more specifically, doubt: *Will God provide for my every financial need?* My question is common to moms as we are often aware of any perceived gaps in need and the resources to meet the need. In fact, most of our questions are rooted in one core question: *Will God provide?*

Will God provide a safe surgery and help me process the results?
Will God provide the healing I need?
Will God provide comfort when I say goodbye to a friend?
Will God provide for my unborn child?
Will God provide for my children's needs?
Will God provide protection against the storm and guard my heart and mind?
Will God provide answers to the questions in my heart?
Will God provide forgiveness when I hurt others or when others hurt me?

The above list of "Will God provide?" questions came from friends' social media posts. Their spoken and unspoken questions reveal the cries of our mama's heart in various seasons. God's answers affirm all that He says He is, for He promises He will supply everything we need "according to His riches in glory by Christ Jesus" (Philippians 4:19). Because of who God is and what Christ did for us, God's Spirit, the Holy Spirit, can work in our hearts, minds, and lives and give us what we need.

God stops our spiraling thoughts and the enemy's triggers. He declares that He is our Provider. God supplies and provides for our needs.

Our Father-daughter connection confirms what God says. Our hearts can trust Him. He is our Help, our Healer, our Comforter, our Answer, our Refuge, and our Redeemer. God is our Provider in whatever shape or form of provision we need.

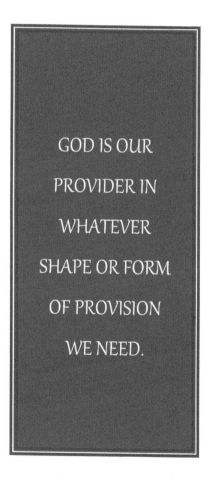

GOD IS OUR

PROVIDER IN

WHATEVER

SHAPE OR FORM

OF PROVISION

WE NEED.

Reflect and Receive

I shared that my trigger is provision represented by the question: Will God provide for my every financial need? The enemy activates my trigger daily. What about you? What is your provision trigger?

_____

_____

_____

_____

_____

_____

_____

_____

_____

_____

_____

_____

_____

_____

_____

_____

_____

_____

_____

God wants you to trust Him. Who He is and His history of faithful provision should earn your trust. What areas do you need to trust God more? Ask God to show you what trusting Him looks like.

_____

_____

_____

_____

_____

_____

_____

_____

_____

_____

_____

_____

_____

_____

Think about your closest friends. What needs for provision do they have? Take some time and pray for your friends and ask God to help the people you love.

_____

_____

_____

_____

_____

_____

_____

_____

_____

_____

_____

_____

_____

_____

_____

_____

_____

_____

_____

_____

_____

_____

_____

Prayer

God, You not only give me a spot before Your throne for my needs, but You make it possible for me to carry others' burdens to You. Thank You for loving all your children—those that know You and those that don't know You yet. God, if there is anything I can do to help others, please prompt me and give me opportunities to say "Yes!" and respond to Your request. Thank You, God, for your generosity and the many ways You gave and continue to give to me.

Verse 17

Behold, God *is* my salvation, I will trust and not be afraid;
"For YAH, the LORD, *is* my strength and song; He also has
become my salvation." (Isaiah 12:2)

God Saves

The relationship we have with God is defined by salvation. God *is* our salvation and He *becomes* our salvation. God sent Jesus to die for our sins and reestablish our connection to Him (*is* salvation). God also, within His relationship with us, *continues to save us* from the effects of sin on our soul and from the chaos and confusion of storms in our everyday lives (*becomes* salvation).

Because of who God is and becomes for us, we can trust Him and not be afraid. God's track record is impeccable. We receive every good thing from God and we rejoice and celebrate who God is. His very name, YAH, is the name we mention when we say, "Hallelujah" and praise Him for all He does.

God is our strength because there are many times when we do not feel strong and our mama's hearts are weakened by the demands of our life. God is our song because there are days when we don't want to sing. There are days when we don't want to praise and the words on our lips and the song in our heart is worry and fear. In these times, God is our song. Zephaniah 3:17 creates a beautiful visual of God singing over us:

The LORD your God in your midst,
The Mighty One, will save;
He will rejoice over you with gladness,
He will quiet you with His love,
He will rejoice over you with singing.

God never looks at our fears and makes fun of us. God doesn't laugh at our tears. The Father heart of God cradles the mama's heart in us and quiets us with His love. God soothes us so we can trust and not be afraid. God rejoices over who we are and His method of rejoicing over our salvation is a song and singing.

Reflect and Receive

What is God's song for you? Is it words? Is it art? Is it something you write or speak? Take some time and ask God to show you what tangible things represent His song for you. What makes your mama's heart "sing"?

_____

_____

_____

_____

_____

_____

_____

_____

_____

_____

_____

_____

_____

_____

_____

_____

_____

_____

_____

_____

_____

God rejoices over you, His child. Take time to rejoice over Him and tell Him what you are thankful for.

_____   _____
_____   _____
_____   _____
_____   _____
_____   _____
_____   _____
_____   _____
_____   _____
_____   _____
_____   _____
_____   _____
_____   _____
_____   _____
_____   _____
_____   _____
_____   _____
_____   _____
_____   _____
_____   _____
_____   _____
_____   _____
_____   _____

Prayer

Thank You, God, for the way You engage me with songs and art and the beauty of Your creation. You are a good Father and I trust in you. In Jesus's name. Amen.

Verse 18

A woman who has friends must herself be friendly, but
there is a friend who sticks closer than a brother.

(Proverbs 18:24 emphasis added)

My Friend

Have you ever thought about how difficult friendships are? I know I have. If I'm transparent, I struggled for a long time to maintain friendships. At the core of who I was I felt rejected and left out. I was certain no one truly wanted to be my friend, so I was feisty and prickly enough to ensure that what I thought would be was exactly what I would experience. If I could reject before I would be rejected, then I wasn't really rejected and I had protected myself.

The enemy had no desire for my mama's heart to have real conversations with other women. He knew that as soon as I began to connect and communicate and compare stories that I would see his same lies, his same deception, and his same tricks again and again. He knew that if I was united with others who experienced common struggles and common desires to be amazing women, wonderful moms, and fabulous wives that something would happen within me. *Together*, we would be stronger. When one of us could not stand, we would help each other out. When one of us needed prayer, the rest of us would pray. We wouldn't allow the enemy to gain traction in our friend's life without a fight. No way. The enemy knows he has no power when God's design reigns in our lives. And he tried to prevent this from happening in my life.

God created the desire for friendship within us because He wants relationship with us. The first thing God did with Adam and Eve in the garden of Eden was connect with them and talk with them. God invested in their lives and God invests in our lives. He is the friend that sticks closer than a brother (Proverbs 18:24). Said another way, we are bonded for life by a connection deeper than shared blood and shared likeliness. We are part of God and He is part of us. He designed us to be in relationship with others and with Him.

The friendship He provides takes the pressure of others away. They don't have to be our everything because *God* is our everything. No matter how much we love or others love, we can't out-do God's love. God is perfect and He loves us perfectly and completely. As amazing as my friends are, they aren't perfect in their love for me and I'm not definitely not perfect in the love I give them. God's expectations are not for us to try to be Him, but to be ourselves. His love for us gives us the courage to let our guard down and be open to friendships. God's presence in our lives provides what we need to be friendly. God gives us what we need to live lives connected to others and to Him, and above all else, to remember that He is that friend who sticks closer than a brother.

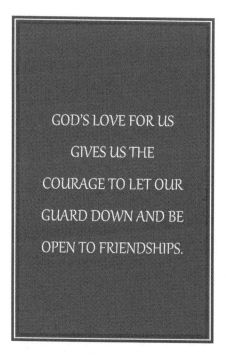

GOD'S LOVE FOR US GIVES US THE COURAGE TO LET OUR GUARD DOWN AND BE OPEN TO FRIENDSHIPS.

Reflect and Receive

Think about your <u>best</u> friendships through the years. What made/makes them so great? How were you loved, accepted, and appreciated by them? How have you loved, accepted, and appreciated others?

_____

_____

_____

_____

_____

_____

_____

_____

_____

_____

_____

_____

_____

_____

_____

_____

_____

_____

_____

God designed us to be in relationships and modeled friendship for us by being a friend to us before we were friends with Him. Romans 5:10 says, "For if when we were enemies we were reconciled to God through the death of His Son, much more, having been reconciled, we shall be saved by His life." Knowing that we once thought, believed, and lived as God's enemies should tell us something about the love God pours out to us to give to others. We don't have to be enemies with anyone. God is the way for us to be friendly to others. Ask God to show you relationships where you struggle with being friendly (much less friends) and to reveal ways He models a better example of friendship.

_____

_____

_____

_____

_____

_____

_____

_____

_____

_____

_____

_____

_____

_____

_____

_____

Our friendship with God and our friendships with others play a key role in healing our mama's heart. The enemy wants to destroy our friendships because he knows we are stronger together than we are on our own. Ask God to give you ways to better invest in your friendships and be friendly to your friends.

_____

_____

_____

_____

_____

_____

_____

_____

_____

_____

_____

_____

_____

_____

_____

_____

_____

_____

_____

_____

Prayer

God, You are the best Father and You teach me everything I need to know about being a good friend. You know the important role friends have in a person's life, and I thank You for allowing me opportunities to both be a friend and to have friends. Help me love others with the love you have given me. In Jesus's name. Amen.

Verse 19

These things I have spoken to you, that in Me you may have peace. In the world you will have tribulation; but be of good cheer, I have overcome the world. (John 16:33)

Jesus Overcomes the World

God knew there would be days that would seem never-ending and horrible to us. He knew that there would be moments that would break our mama's heart, and sink our confidence. God knew that we would experience the worst of the worst at times, and our experiences would leave us feeling certain of our defeat.

There is nothing easy that God calls us to when He gives us a mama's heart. He knew before He gave us the desire to love as a mom loves that we would feel rejection and feel inadequate. He knew we would compare ourselves with each other—against His advice—and never measure up as highly as we'd like. God knows us. He also knows this world we live in. He knows the guts it takes to maneuver through the muck of any given day and He enables us with the strength we need. We can't do what God has called us to do without Him.

He is not ignorant of our struggles. God is all-knowing and He knows all about us and the difficulties we face in our everyday lives. He tells us that the peace we seek and the peace we need we have in Him. Without God, we won't find peace in the report cards our kids bring home, the people they date, or the choices they make. God steadies our hearts and empowers us.

The enemy loves to use the world as a glaring example of all that could go wrong with us and our families. The world the enemy tries to tempt us to disengage and distance ourselves from is exactly the place that God sets up camp. God fights for us and wins our battles every time.

The world the enemy tries tempt us to see as chaotic and a threat, God says is His—and that He is in control of it. God wins, every time. Because of the victory we have in God, we can be in the world, in the middle of chaos, and have peace and be of good cheer. Or to put it another way, we can be *in* the world but not *of* the world. While the world hates us we can be at peace, because God loves us and He has overcome the world.

GOD

WINS,

EVERY

TIME.

Reflect and Receive

God wants you to know that He is in control. Though the world you are in may seem out of control, God is never out of control—nor does He leave you with chaos. You have peace in Him. Ask God to show you how He transforms chaos into order and gives you strength.

_____

_____

_____

_____

_____

_____

_____

_____

_____

_____

_____

_____

_____

_____

_____

_____

_____

_____

The enemy can't defeat you, but he can convince you that you are defeated. The enemy can lie to you and tell you that you don't have hope in your current situation. The awesome news is the enemy does not win, not once. God wins every time. Ask God to show you how He has won the victory in your life and how He gives you peace.

_____

_____

_____

_____

> ## THE ENEMY DOES NOT WIN, NOT ONCE.

_____

_____

_____

_____

_____

_____

_____

_____

_____

_____

_____

When people are stressed or in a messy situation, what they think and say about themselves can deteriorate quickly to the point that they often communicate things about themselves that they would never say to or about anyone else. Ask God if you are your own worst enemy and let Him reveal more of how He sees you, loves you, and gives you hope and strength.

_____

_____

_____

_____

_____

_____

_____

_____

_____

_____

_____

_____

_____

_____

_____

_____

_____

_____

_____

_____

_____

_____

Prayer

God, thank You for the way You guard my heart and mind through Christ Jesus. You redeem my faults and failures and the faults and failures of those around me. You give me strength and hope. You give me a peace that passes my understanding (Philippians 4:7) and this makes me strong and resilient in You. Thank You for who You are and who I am becoming in You.

Verse 20

Then he said to them, "Go your way, eat the fat, drink the sweet, and send portions to those for whom nothing is prepared; for this day is holy to our Lord. Do not sorrow, for the joy of the Lord is your strength." (Nehemiah 8:10)

Joy & Strength

Do you know that God gave you permission to be yourself? This verse reminds me of how God designed us to celebrate who we are to Him no matter what is going on around us. God gives us the strength we need to rejoice even when we don't feel like rejoicing. When we hear bad news or experience realities that sadden our mama's heart, the joy of the Lord is our strength.

When I first read that verse, the part that resonated with me was "and send portions to those for whom nothing is prepared." I've been a mom ill-prepared in both good times and bad times. I've been taken by surprise and caught off-guard without everything ready to go . . . many times!

I've been the mom who sent my then third-grade daughter to school dressed as Wonder Woman . . . *on the wrong day*. I've been the mom who forgot field trip slips and lunches and cringed when my kids did the same. I've been the mom who spoke angry words that hurt my child and I had to watch the hurt and sadness rise in my child's eyes as I had to say, "I'm sorry."

More times than I care to admit I've been a mom who could have been grieved by the *law* pushing upon my mama's heart telling me how much I do wrong. But instead, God gave me joy and strength through His grace and He told me how He made everything right.

I am sure there have been times where you missed the mark also. God speaks into our situations and says, "I AM" and that is enough. When God tells us who we are, we should listen. Even though it might boggle our minds to think of ourselves as highly as He does, we can trust the Father's heart.

The words God speaks over us again and again in our relationship with Him are words of life. He breathes life into us and we become the living souls He designed us to be. No matter what is going on, today is a day to hold fast to the Lord and His love for you. You are not defeated but instead a warrior with the battle already credited to you. The joy of the Lord is your strength.

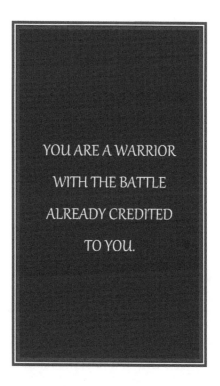

YOU ARE A WARRIOR

WITH THE BATTLE

ALREADY CREDITED

TO YOU.

Reflect and Receive

There is only one you. God designed you for a unique identity as His daughter, to thrive in relationship with Him and in a purpose that He gives. He designed you to celebrate who He, is no matter what you experience. Take some time and thank God for who He is.

_____

_____

_____

_____

_____

_____

_____

_____

_____

_____

_____

_____

_____

The only person you can truly become is the person God made you to be. God did not make you by mistake or poor design. If you grieve who you are or wish you were different, talk to God and ask Him for words to define you that allow His joy to be your strength.

_____

_____

_____

_____

_____

_____

_____

_____

_____

_____

_____

_____

_____

_____

_____

_____

_____

_____

_____

_____

_____

Prayer

God, I am grateful for how You equip me for every good work in You. From my relationship with You, I can become whom You created me to be. God, if I in any way believe a lie that You somehow made a mistake in who I am, would You tell me the truth and speak words of life to me? Thank You for being the Daddy You are and setting me on the adventure You designed for me. I am Your beloved daughter on an incredible journey. Thank You for being You.

Purpose

Verse 21

The Lord is with you, Mighty Warrior.

(Judges 6:12 NIV)

Raising Warriors

When my first child was born, I received multiple copies of a popular book on parenting strong-willed children. When my second child was born, I received more copies of this book. After the birth of my third child I had a friend remark, "You seem to only give birth to one type of child." What she said did not minimize the uniqueness of my children as they have very different personalities, interests, and strengths; she observed a quality about them, me, and my husband that, as different as we are, we had in common. "It's like you all are chiefs and you gave birth to little chiefs." I loved her description as she was correct. In many ways, I gave birth to what I am as that is God's design.

God designed us to embody certain qualities and traits that we pass on to those who call us mom in whatever sense of that treasured title is ours. God fills the mama's heart with the equipment of a Warrior because for us to be the moms God calls us to be we must see ourselves the way God sees us.

God is incredibly good at calling things that are not as though they are. He is Creator. He calls into existence and gives life to the dead (Romans 4:17). He declares who we are and with all He says comes a Divine purpose.

As I was writing this devotion I was stuck and unsure what to write. I wanted to tell you about Gideon and how God called Him a mighty warrior when He wasn't one yet. At that moment my friend, Valen, texted me the verse above. Talk about timing! In a moment where I wasn't feeling very Warrior-esque and sure that writing anything was a terrible idea, she texted me: "The Lord is with you, mighty warrior. Go in the strength you have . . . I will be with you and you will _____." I filled in the blank with "defeat my Midianites." In this case my Midianites were thoughts and ideas trying to revolt against all God is, and what He called me to be.

151

God calls you and me. He tells us we are Mighty Warriors even though we may not feel courageous. He assures us that the battles we must fight we can fight with the strength He gives us—and that He will be with us. Our relationship with God declares that confidence into our purpose.

Reflect and Receive

God has called you a warrior in Christ. This does not mean that you need to fight your own battles, but that God fights for you and with you in a battle He has already won. Ask God to show you how He uniquely equipped you to be a warrior in God's kingdom who trains up warriors.

_____

_____

_____

_____

_____

_____

_____

_____

_____

_____

_____

_____

_____

_____

_____

_____

_____

_____

_____

Every gift in God's kingdom can be marginalized and explained from a physical view. Often, characteristics about God's people that are strengths in God's kingdom are described in ways and with thoughts, feelings, and emotions that are not honoring. "Strong-willed" is often used in a negative way when God designed a gift of strength to be good. Ask God if there are terms used about you or your children that need to be reclaimed for His purposes.

Does the word "warrior" God uses to describe you seem to fit? Ask God to show you how the description applies to you.

_____

_____

_____

_____

_____

_____

_____

_____

_____

_____

_____

_____

_____

_____

_____

_____

_____

_____

_____

_____

_____

_____

_____

_____

Prayer

God, thank You for showing me that my battle is not against flesh and blood. I don't fight people and You fight for me and with me. God, You give me courage and strength to trust You and listen to Your voice. You are faithful and You promise to lead me and guide me for your name's sake. I praise You for who You are. In Jesus's name. Amen.

Verse 22

Imitate me, just as I also imitate Christ.

(1 Corinthians 11:1)

Next Generation

To be honest, there have been times when I regretted that my children followed my example. I made a mistake and they made the same mistake. "Follow me" doesn't always look like strength. Sometimes "follow me" means our kids see us not at our best and more human that we'd like. In those times, "follow me" means we admit we were wrong and seek their forgiveness.

"Follow me" always means that to be the moms God designed us to be we should follow Christ. Following Christ means we rely on God, trust Him, claim His promises, and rest in His absolutes. One of those promises and absolutes that we follow and teach our children to follow is that God is faithful; He never leaves us or forsakes us. When God pronounces that He provides for our every need, He provides for our every need. When God declares His lovingkindness never fails and His compassion or mercies are renewed each morning, He means what He says.

When we represent God or imitate Christ, we don't generate some crazy letter-of-the-law life. Instead, we look at the way Christ lived and the way He loved. Christ operated from perfect positioning within the Father's heart. His reaction to situations and circumstances and His relationships with others were without sin (Hebrews 4:15). He sat with people no one else wanted to sit with and talked with people declared unclean and not worthy. He healed people and did the work of His Father who sent Him.

Because Christ paid the final price for sin, we can live a redemptive life in a recreated story. We can live a life without regrets doing the work of the Father who loves us. We can reflect the love Christ had and God gives and operate in the Spirit of God.

When we are who we are created to be, we make it easier for our kids—biological, adopted, and spiritual—to see themselves as God created them to be. They have courage because of our courage in Christ. They have strength because of our strength from God. They are loved as we are loved. They learn to imitate Christ just as we imitate Christ and follow Him.

WHEN WE ARE WHO WE ARE CREATED TO BE, WE MAKE IT EASIER TO FOR OUR KIDS TO SEE THEMSELVES AS GOD CREATED THEM TO BE.

Reflect and Receive

The enemy lies and will tell you that your influence and impact on your kids' lives is minimal. The truth is, they watch you more than you realize and they process and receive more than you probably believe they do. Ask God to show you how your words inspire your children to follow Him.

_____

_____

_____

_____

_____

_____

_____

_____

_____

_____

_____

_____

_____

_____

_____

_____

Telling another person to "follow me as I follow Christ" can be intimidating and challenging. How does that phrase "follow me as I follow Christ," encourage you to rely on God more?

_____

_____

_____

_____

_____

_____

_____

_____

_____

_____

_____

_____

_____

_____

_____

_____

_____

_____

Prayer

God, help me be a person who relies on You and follows You. I can't be the mom You designed me to be of my own will. Teach me how to imitate You more. Help me to view You from the perspective of grace and life, and not law and death. Give me the words to teach my children about You.

Verse 23

For *she* shall be like a tree planted by the waters, which spreads out its roots by the river, And will not fear when heat comes; But its leaf will be green, And will not be anxious in the year of drought, Nor will cease from yielding fruit. (Jeremiah 17:8, emphasis added)

Like a Tree Planted

God created us to be like the tree Jeremiah wrote of—near life-giving water with deep roots to draw nourishment from and have the stability we need, with no fear of the heat, with green leaves, not anxious in difficult times, and continually yielding fruit.

We are like that tree. When our lives don't reflect what God has for us, there is a problem with our beliefs. We don't believe we are like that tree so what we see matches the limits of our beliefs.

If I see a large electric bill that is much more expensive than I planned and budgeted for, and I believe that there won't be money to pay that bill, there won't be money to pay that bill. However, if I believe God is who He says He is—and He said that He would provide for my every need—God will provide for that bill. My beliefs did not limit what God wanted to reveal in the situation.

To be who God declared you to be and fully engage in the purpose He declared you to be engaged in, you need to believe in who He says *you* are. You are His daughter and He loves you; God has every good thing for you. God protects your mama's heart and helps your unbelief. He tells you that you are His beloved child and you have what you need, you have no need to fear, you have life, you don't have anything to be anxious about, and you will produce fruit. In other words, you have nothing to lose. What God has for you is done and won for you.

God's words to us are promises that He has fulfilled and faithfully will fulfill. As He speaks from His Father's heart to our mama's heart, He gives us hope for the future we have in Him and a future full of life that never stops producing fruit.

Reflect and Receive

Jeremiah 17:8 declares you are like a tree planted by the waters; this truth makes it easy to overlook God's provision to you. You are nourished by God. All God does for you allows you to be as He created and designed. A tree doesn't work to be a tree; it is a tree and as a tree it merely draws from the water and nutrition from soil and *is* as God created. Ask God to show you how He made you like the tree in that verse to reflect His design—and how He created you to *be*, not a person that needs to *do*.

Moms believe in good for themselves and their kids. God wants to give you, as a mom, exactly that. He gives you good gifts, by design, as your good Father. If there is an area of your life you feel you are lacking in, which—if God provided—would give you the strength to bear fruit no matter what, ask God to show you how He already has given you what you need.

Prayer

God, it is incredibly humbling to see myself through Your eyes and I am grateful for Your love, kindness, and tenderness. You cultivate within me a sweetness and strength that can only come to me from who You are. You raise me up to be strong, bold, and brave. Thank You, God, for giving me Your strength and for guiding me in the path and purpose You have for me. I love you for all You are.

Verse 24

Behold, I will do a new thing, now it shall spring forth;

Shall you not know it? I will even make a road in the

wilderness and rivers in the desert. (Isaiah 43:19)

God Does a New Thing

God wants us to trust Him even when it is difficult. God knows who we are and He knows our tendencies to shy away from the new and stick to the comfort of what we know. New can be uncomfortable. Moms are a strong lot and our mama's heart can be a force. God knows this about us because He created these strengths within us. He knows that new is difficult at times to embrace. New can be scary, and we can feel vulnerable and unsure in a different place as God does a new thing. God knows our concerns and He invites us to trust Him and what He is doing in our lives.

He tells us that what He is doing will spring forth. This means we will likely suspect, but not really know, what God is doing as He is doing it. What God is doing may catch us by surprise, but we can trust God because what God brings is life. As we walk where God leads, He makes things new for us and we will know where He is at work. Relationship with God creates familiarity with God. We know God, see God, and follow God.

Scripture affirms that God does not change (Numbers 23:19), and since God changes not, we can expect Him to lead us in a way we can trust and that is for our good. The more we experience the Father's heart, the more we will know the Father's heart in a new set of circumstances. Instead of being afraid we will be able to trust God and follow where He leads.

God promises that He will make a road in the wilderness. That means where there wasn't a way there is one now—and it was God who prepared that way. We didn't have to dig, scrape, or crawl our way through; God made a way.

When God creates a way for us—revealing His purpose to us—sustainability results. God gives the resources that bring life and supply for needs. He may move in a direction He has never moved before and do something new to us and for us, but God's methods and ways are not changing; we can trust in Him. How God will do a new thing in your life most likely will not resemble how He does a new thing in my life, but every step of the way He will show us that we can trust Him, we can know Him, we will know His way, and His way will bring life.

Reflect and Receive

God is making a way in your life. Ask Him to show you where He is doing a new thing.

_____

_____

_____

_____

_____

_____

_____

_____

_____

_____

_____

_____

_____

_____

_____

_____

_____

_____

_____

Do new things make you uncomfortable? Ask God to remind you of the times He made ways for you before.

_____

_____

_____

_____

_____

_____

_____

_____

_____

_____

_____

_____

_____

_____

_____

God made and makes ways.

Prayer

God, thank You for the ways You made for me to connect to you and see you and see others and connect to them. I see you through Christ and I see the world through You. Thank you for showing me the world that needs to know who you are. Thank You for giving me the words to describe You and Your love for me. Thank You for making me the beloved daughter I am.

Verse 25

There is neither Jew nor Greek, there is neither slave nor free, there is neither male nor female; for you are all one in Christ Jesus. (Galatians 3:28)

God Gives Equality

In Christ there are no longer man-made definitions. We aren't defined by our gender, jobs, or titles. Whether we biologically have children or not doesn't matter. God's purpose was to unify all that He created in His image for an uncommon work. According to Galatians 3:26, those who believe in Jesus have become "sons" in Christ: "For you are all sons of God through faith in Christ Jesus. For as many of you as were baptized into Christ have put on Christ" (Galatians" 3:26–27).

Every promise in Scripture to sons is a promise to daughters. We, as daughters, are not exempt or excluded from all that Christ died to restore to us. We, made in the image of God, have a Divine purpose given to use by an infallible God. God did not make a mistake when He gave you a mama's heart. A mama's heart is a place of connection with God. Through the mama's heart we receive the God's truth. The mama's heart contains God's love, and from the healed mama's heart, we reflect Christ and invite others to imitate or follow Christ as we imitate and follow Him.

As women, we reveal who God is through who we are in Christ. We have equal opportunity and equal responsibility to present the gospel of Jesus to the world who needs Him. God created all of us to be in community and connection with Him. Second Peter 3:9 says, "The Lord is not slack concerning His promise, as some count slackness, but is longsuffering toward us, not willing that any should perish but that all should come to repentance." God wants all people to come to know Him and invites people of every gender, job, and title to experience the connection with Him that we have through Christ.

All people need Christ, God, and the Holy Spirit. We are simply not who we are created to be without acknowledging Christ's salvation, God's purpose, and the Holy Spirit's presence in our everyday lives.

God's uncommon work is our salvation and redemption and He invites all of us into the process as sons of God.

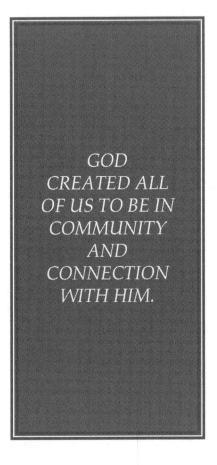

GOD CREATED ALL OF US TO BE IN COMMUNITY AND CONNECTION WITH HIM.

Reflect and Receive

God is inviting you to join Him in sharing His story through your life. Ask God to give you the words to His story in your life. This is your personal testimony. This is the story of how God healed your mama's heart as He gave you identity, relationship, and purpose in Him

_____

_____

_____

_____

_____

_____

_____

_____

_____

_____

_____

_____

_____

_____

_____

_____

_____

_____

Prayer

God, there is nothing more effective than talking about how You work in my life, and what You did to bring about my salvation story. Thank You for giving me the words to share Your story at work in my life. Help my testimony encourage others to see You and follow You more. In Jesus's name. Amen.

Verse 26

The Lord will fight for you, and you shall hold your peace.

(Exodus 14:14)

Why God Fights for You

There have been many times where I wondered why God fought so hard for me. Why did He save me from my own choices? Why did He physically heal my body from cancer and disease? Why did He give me chance after chance after chance to accept that He wanted a relationship with me? Why did He try so hard to show me that He loved me when I fought Him and pushed Him away?

The simple answer is: You.

If God had given up on me, you and I would have never met you through this devotional, this devotional would have never been written, and likely I would be dead. I am grateful God kept fighting for me. I also grateful that He fought for you. If my story includes such battles to bring me to this place, I know yours was a struggle also. As I write those words, all I can see are God's hands on us and His protection over us, drawing us to this place. He speaks to both of us and tells us what He has likely told us before: *He fights for us.* God fights our battles so we don't have to. We have victory in Him. Because He has already won, any battle we fight is *from* victory not *for* victory.

When God fights for us He tells us to be still, to hold our peace. What comes against us is not from the physical realm, even though the fight may seem physical and personal. It comes from the spiritual realm. Because of this, we don't fight the battle with physical weapons, "For we do not wrestle against flesh and blood, but against principalities, against powers, against the rulers of the darkness of this age, against spiritual hosts of wickedness in the heavenly places" (Ephesians 6:12). A spiritual battle looks a bit different from a physical battle; in it we can hold our peace or be still because the Lord fights for us and He wins the battle every time.

Reflect and Receive

When God fights battles, the battle is different. Your natural response may be to *do* something to fight what you see as the problem—and the problem you see may often be a person. However, God says that your *real* battle is not against flesh and blood. The enemy wants nothing more than to see you fight the wrong battle and have your mama's heart hurt in the process.

Ask God what your battle really is and ask Him how He fights for you.

_____

_____

_____

_____

_____

_____

_____

_____

_____

_____

_____

_____

_____

_____

_____

_____

Holding your peace or being still is incredibly difficult to do. Human beings are wired to act. Being still, however, is a response to trusting God. Holding your peace does not mean nothing is being done but that God is doing everything to fight your battle for you. Ask God to help you see what holding your peace and being still looks like.

Prayer

God, help me be still and see You are at work in my life. You fight my battles and You lead me in the perfect response every time. God, I don't see what You see or know what You know; teach me to trust You more and listen for Your voice. You love me and You protect me. In Jesus's name. Amen.

Verse 27

God sets the solitary in families; He brings out those who are

bound into prosperity; But the rebellious dwell in

a dry land. (Psalm 68:6)

God Gives Moms to the Lonely

Being lonely or feeling alone is an incredible and destructive lie of the enemy. God knew that freedom happens in families and He designed a way for those who are lonely or feel alone to be in a family. This opportunity to be part of a family utilizes the mama's heart through the lives of biological, adopted, or spiritual mamas.

Biological mamas are the physical mamas who gave birth to another individual. An adopted mama is a person who is mom to a child that they did not give birth to but who became their child through legal process. A spiritual mama is *any* woman who has adopted *any* individual for the God-led purpose of teaching, instructing, encouraging, directing, building, or in some way equipping them to do the work of God's kingdom. A spiritual mama could also be the biological or adopted mom to a child, but she does not *have* to be.

We all need a mom and most of us, throughout our unique freedom journeys, need more than one mama in our life. God meets our needs. He gave us the physical mom who gave birth to us. To some, He gave an adopted mom to raise us. But He also gives us other women—spiritual mamas—who teach us key truths that we need to know.

God uses every avenue He can to ensure that people are not alone and that they can learn more about who He is inside of the mama's heart. Despite His provision, there are many mamas who refuse to embrace the role of the mama's heart and there are many "children" who refuse to embrace the mamas God gave them. The reality of this rejection of the family God provides is death, not life; bondage and not freedom.

God not only gives moms to the lonely, but He gives the lonely to moms. In a beautiful exchange designed as only He can design, God often uses the experiences and strengths of one woman's heart to heal another's heart because, "God is not willing that any should perish but that all should come to repentance" (2 Peter 3:9). The way God connects us to Him is often through each other and the families He creates and provides for us.

> THE WAY GOD CONNECTS US TO HIM IS OFTEN THROUGH EACH OTHER AND THE FAMILIES HE CREATES AND PROVIDES FOR US.

Reflect and Receive

All women are wired for connection. God put your lonely heart in families—as both a mama (biological, adopted and/or spiritual) and as a child (biological, adopted and/or spiritual).

Take some time to identify your families. To determine who are your children, list your biological and/or adopted children and decide, based upon the criteria above, if you are also their spiritual mama (likely you are). Also identify others—not your biological or adopted children—whom you have a mother-like or mentor relationship with. Ask God to show you what your spiritual relationship is with each of these people if you are not sure.

Just as you are someone's mama, you are likely someone's child. List your biological mom, adopted mom, stepmom, aunts, women who mentor you, moms of your friends, or other women in leadership who speak into your life. Ask God to show you how each of these women uniquely help you understand who God created you to be.

_____
_____
_____
_____
_____
_____
_____
_____
_____
_____
_____
_____
_____
_____
_____
_____
_____
_____
_____
_____
_____
_____

Sometimes God gives women spiritual mamas or spiritual children for distinct reasons and seasons in their lives. If there is someone that met the criteria of spiritual mama or spiritual child previously, but not now, list them here and ask God to help you define what their role was in your life. If you need to grieve the loss of "a mama" or "a child," let God comfort you.

_____

_____

_____

_____

_____

_____

_____

_____

_____

_____

_____

_____

_____

_____

_____

_____

_____

_____

_____

_____

Prayer

What a beautiful plan You made to set my lonely heart in different families. God, thank You for the women You have blessed me with throughout my life as both a mama and a spiritual mama. Thank You for the unique way they showed me more of who You are and the freedom You have for me. God, thank You for entrusting the hearts of Your children to me as a mama and a spiritual mama. By your example, You have shown me how to nurture, love, and carefully handle Your child's heart. God, may You continue to use Your families to bring freedom to me and to them. I love You and am grateful for all You do through the name of Jesus and by the power of Your Spirit at work within me. Thank You, God! In Jesus's name. Amen.

Verse 28

Older women similarly are to be reverent in their behavior, not malicious gossips nor addicted to much wine, teaching what is right and good. (Titus 2:3 AMP)

Mamas Teach

God designed the mama's heart for conversation and constructive teaching. His way is what is represented within Titus 2. As His children are placed within families, the older teach the younger. Older here may not always be represented by a physical age but a spiritual maturity. I have had spiritual mamas my age or barely older, and I have been a spiritual mama to women new in their faith but much older than me.

We need instruction and wisdom in our everyday lives and God blesses us with women rooted in Christ who listen to God, operate within the body of Christ, model reverent behavior, exhibit honorable actions, abstain from addicting habits, and who can teach us "what is right and good" (Titus 2:3). Their mama's heart activates and serves within God's family to show younger women (in age or spiritual maturity) how to love their husbands and children.

What God constructed within His family was designed to heal hearts within one generation and give us the way of victorious living. God put our hearts in families to train the next generation to know their identity, seek relationship, and live free in His purpose to share the gospel of Christ and be who they are created to be. What God designed is incredibly simple, yet effective.

A mama's heart awakened and healed from hurt receives God and relates with others beautifully. As God heals our mama's heart, He gives each of us the ability to share who He is with other children in His family. God heals us so we can be utilized in others' healing. God frees us so we can be free people who free people.

God designed the mama's heart to—in the most life-giving and uncomplicated way—connect to Him and others, and teach what is beneficial to others within God's family.

Reflect and Receive

God will use your story and the power of your testimony to write on others' hearts. Second Corinthians 3:2–3 beautifully speaks to this process and who you are in Christ:

> You are our epistle written in our hearts, known and read by all men; clearly you are an epistle of Christ, ministered by us, written not with ink but by the Spirit of the living God, not on tablets of stone but on tablets of flesh, that is, of the heart.

You are the story of Christ that ministers to others. Your mama's heart contains the treasure of who God says you are and all He prepared for you to do. The treasure within you brings life within His family and connection with the body of Christ. Ask Him about your story within the body of Christ.

_____

_____

_____

_____

_____

_____

_____

_____

_____

_____

_____

_____

Prayer

God, You define who I am. I praise You that I am fearfully and wonderfully made (Psalm 139:14). Thank You for the story of Christ that You wrote on my heart and designed to be shared with others. I praise You for who You are and I am grateful for who You created me to be.

Verse 29

When I call to remembrance the unfeigned faith that is in thee, which dwelt first in thy grandmother Lois, and thy mother Eunice; and I am persuaded that is in thee also.

(2 Timothy 1:5)

The Legacy of a Mama's Heart

The lady I call Mrs. Jones was in my life for a brief time and a specific reason. Our church family visited her as part of ministry and one day we had a picnic at her house. She and I sat side by side on her porch swing; I was five, and she was ancient. I watched Mrs. Jones as she stared at the sea of people with a proud, loving look. As she watched them talk or play yard games, I inched my arm closer to hers. Mrs. Jones and I looked very different. My arm was small, thin, and pale, and her arm was strong, petite, and much darker than mine. When our arms finally touched, Mrs. Jones realized what I was doing. She looked at our two arms side by side and laughed this delicious laugh that bubbled from somewhere deep within her. "You and I do look different, but in our hearts, we are the same. God loves us both."

I smiled and snuggled next to her and she wrapped her arms around me. We continued to watch people celebrate God and each other inside this diverse family. She said all my heart needed to know about our differences, and all I truly cared about, was that we were the same. Mrs. Jones may have had more input and influence in my life than this singular event; however, I don't recall any other time where Mrs. Jones's mama's heart ministered to mine as she did that day when she and I sat side-by-side on her porch swing.

When I remember her real, genuine faith, I believe in the truth she told me and that I knew was in me: she and I were the same. We were connected at the spirit level, and God loved us both.

You have your own Mrs. Jones or Mrs. Smith or Mrs. _____ who spoke to you maybe once or maybe throughout your life. These spiritual mamas live out the legacy of faith through their mama's heart to yours. They show you who God was, who God is, and who God will be through His relationship with us, His children. Their unfeigned faith—real faith—is rooted in righteousness received from Christ, and not in anything they do or we do but in what God has done. In Timothy's life, we see a multi-generational legacy of living for God. For some, we are the first in our family to see ourselves as a beloved daughter of God. For us, Christ gave us a new family tree overflowing with a great legacy of faith. We are new creations in Christ and old things have passed away (2 Corinthians 5:17). That means spiritually speaking we are all first generation. We are sons and daughters of God, joint heirs with Christ (Romans 8:17). God is doing something new; He makes a family with a mama's heart, and connects her heart to others through faith.

GOD MAKES A FAMILY WITH A MAMA'S HEART, AND CONNECTS HER HEART TO OTHERS THROUGH FAITH.

Reflect and Receive

Write out your legacy of faith. What were some key moments with your spiritual mamas that helped define who God is and who you are?

_____

_____

_____

_____

_____

_____

_____

_____

_____

_____

_____

_____

_____

_____

_____

_____

_____

_____

_____

_____

Prayer

God, thank You for the many ways You have spoken into my life through spiritual mamas. You knew what my mama's heart needed long before I knew I had this gift from You. Help me steward well the gift of the mama's heart and use what You have given me to reflect You to others who need You. I am thankful and grateful for all that You establish through the name of Jesus. In Jesus' name. Amen.

Verse 30

But seek first the kingdom of God and His righteousness,

and all these things shall be added to you. (Matthew 6:33)

Seek God First

Our purpose in the kingdom of God is to show who God is and what He has done. This is the purpose God gave us. Teaching faith and connection inside of the body of Christ is what the mama's heart does best. God knew our tendencies to rely on ourselves instead of trusting Him to meet our needs. He gave us mamas—biological, adopted, and spiritual—to teach us about Himself, about who we are as beloved daughters and the purpose God gives to each of us to share what relationship with Him looks like. God heals our mama's heart so we can be part of the healing process within other's lives. He uses the mama's heart to teach us how to trust Him more.

God says that who we are and what we do is not by our might and power but that He saves us according to His Spirit within us, regenerating and renewing us (Titus 3:5). God has "saved us and called us with a holy calling, not according to our works, but according to His own purpose and grace which was given to us in Christ Jesus before time began" (1 Timothy 1:9).

As we seek first the kingdom of God and His righteousness, God will tell us what we need to know and where and how He needs us to function inside of the body of Christ. The same faith that built us builds others. The same faith that brought freedom to us brings freedom to others.

Our mama's heart receives and then gives good gifts from God. All that God gives to us flows through us and to others. God tells us to seek Him so others know how to seek Him. He tells us to ask Him for wisdom for what we don't know so that we can show others how to ask for wisdom. God makes a way for us to trust Him when situations hurt so that we can share that way to others when situations are difficult for them.

God tells us that He will go before us and He will be with us and not leave us or forsake us. We are told to not fear or be dismayed (Deuteronomy 31:8) We are to seek first the kingdom of God and He will provide a purpose, a relationship, and an identity that says we are beloved daughters on an incredible journey.

Reflect and Receive

Take time to reflect on what God showed you about your mama's heart. What did you receive from God that you did not know before?

_____

_____

_____

_____

_____

_____

_____

_____

_____

_____

_____

_____

_____

_____

_____

_____

_____

_____

_____

_____

_____

_____

God connects us to each other and tells us to seek first His kingdom. God's designs are whole, complete, and lack no good thing. Ask God about His kingdom and what seeking His kingdom first looks like.

God celebrates the mama's heart. His joy will bubble up from somewhere deep within you and tell you who He is and who you are. God does not regret anything about you, but celebrates everything. Take more time to ask God to speak to your mama's heart and tell you, again, how much He loves and celebrates who you are.

_____

_____

_____

_____

_____

_____

_____

_____

_____

_____

_____

_____

_____

_____

Prayer

God, the journey of the mama's heart is a journey to Your heart. Thank You for giving me a way to be your beloved daughter. Thank You for the relationship, through Christ, that I have with You. Thank You for Your Spirit, alive and at work within me. I am grateful for how You use my mama's heart in Your redemptive process and how the power of my testimony leads others to see You more. Help me to seek first Your kingdom and know all that You give to me. In Jesus's name. Amen.

Acknowledgments

No writer writes a book alone. I am grateful for the many men and women who helped me reach this writing milestone.

Specifically, I am grateful for my amazing husband, *Mike*, who not only encouraged me every step of the way but made sure the kids and pets were fed and the world kept spinning as I wrote. You are my greatest treasure. With you, the fun is in the journey as much as the destination.

Thank you to *Kayleigh, Andrew* and *Alexa* who have called me a bestselling author long before I was. Each of you have been instrumental to my writing journey and I am thankful I'm your mama!

Mom and Dad, you two gave me a love of words, life and taught me that with God all things are possible. Love you both.

My bonus family, Mom and Dad Hamilton and my stepdaughter, Kaile and her husband, Matt. Many thanks for your prayers and support through the years!

My brother, *David*, you invested first and the most in teaching me to read, spell and told me through the years that I was awesome and amazing. You are the best brother in the world.

To my sweet God-given sisters (specifically *Valen Workman, Lisa Goss, Laura Hill, Katy Seedorf, Wendy Earley, Mary Jo Johnson, Meridith Hall, Kim McAfee, Roselle Joven, Kimberly Volner, Kerry Dale, Svet-Lana Dickens, Rebecca Cornelius* and *Christina Farrah)* you refused to let me be silent. Thank you for calling what I didn't see to life and supporting me as I found my voice. Love you all!

To my spiritual mamas-*Janice Baldwin, Chris Pitt,* and *Leisha Darling*-You've walked with me through some tough identity-finding times and you've stayed by me keeping me accountable to the process of God at work in my life. Thank you, thank you, thank you! Your love and faithfulness are wonderful gifts!

To *Bob and Polly Hamp*, there are simply not enough words. Thank you for your leadership, friendship, love, support and the many ways you challenged me and gave me permission to "think differently". I am a different daughter thanks to you both.

To *John Stickl*, I found my voice because you found yours. Thank you for leading us at Valley Creek Church and starting me on the most incredible journey with "It Is Finished" and teaching me through the years how to *Follow the Cloud* and be a Kingdom leader.

To *Kathy Carlton Willis* and the other *WordGirls-my writer friends who know the ins and outs of the crazy process of birthing a book*-thank you for all the ways you challenged and encouraged me through this year to run my race and be faithful to the process of writing. Thank you!

To *Tony Fiore*, you spoke life and cast vision into my daughter's heart. Thank you for the many ways you taught me to do ministry. Can't wait to join you on the mission field and see God bring more adventures to us both!

To *Ron and Leisha Darling*, from the beginning, you two were different and loved me unconditionally. The two of you spoke into my identity as a writer and beloved daughter more than anyone else these last few years. Love you both!

To my Facebook friends, you've watched as I churned out words and encouraged me to write in more ways than you will ever know. Thank you for the time you took to answer my questions and give feedback. I am grateful for your investment in my life.

To my editor, *Karen Engle,* you made my best better. Thank you!

Finally, to the publishing team at WindSpirit Press, I owe you. You took a chance, cast vision and gave me a role at the heart of God doing a new thing. Thank you for entrusting me with the assignment of "first author" of WindSpirit Press. Excited to see what God will do as we follow Him!

30 Verses to Heal a Mama's Heart

Verse 1

Psalm 16:6

Verse 2

2 Corinthians 5:17

Verse 3

Philippians 4:13

Verse 4

Jeremiah 1:5

Verse 5

Genesis 1:27

Verse 6

Ecclesiastes 7:8

Verse 7

1 John 4:17

Verse 8

John 8:32

Verse 9

Romans 6:4

Verse 10

Exodus 6:7

Verse 11	**Verse 12**
Romans 8:28	John 14:17
Verse 13	**Verse 14**
James 1:17	Psalm 23:3
Verse 15	**Verse 16**
Matthew 11:29	Philippians 4:19
Verse 17	**Verse 18**
Isaiah 12:2	Proverbs 18:24
Verse 19	**Verse 20**
John 16:33	Nehemiah 8:10

Verse 21

Judges 6:12

Verse 22

1 Corinthians 11:1

Verse 23

Jeremiah 17:8

Verse 24

Isaiah 43:19

Verse 25

Galatians 3:28

Verse 26

Exodus 14:14

Verse 27

Psalm 68:6

Verse 28

Titus 2:3

Verse 29

2 Timothy 1:5

Verse 30

Matthew 6:33

Thank you for walking through the first 30 Verses™ devotional.
The next devotional will be released February 2018!

Made in the USA
Columbia, SC
04 December 2017